PMP Exam Prep Streamlined

The Complete Guide to Mastering the Exam on the First Attempt - Featuring a Q&A Practice Test, and 50 Hours of E-Learning Videos

Angel B. Howell

Contents

FREE SUPPLEMENTARY RESOURCES

Boost your PMP exam readiness by utilizing special, no-cost resources - available through the provided QR code.

Embark on your path to PMP exam achievement with our exclusive, free resources available for instant download. Tailored to enrich your comprehension and hone your test-taking skills, these materials are key to attaining a superior level of preparedness.

✔ 50-Hours of E-Learning Videos

✔ 300 Flashcards

✔ 1000 Additional Q&A Practice Tests

✔ 3 Interactive Full-Length Practice Tests

✔ PMP Cheats Sheets

SCAN THE QR CODE TO DOWNLOAD

COMPLEMENTARY RESOURCES

Introduction

Purpose and Significance of the Book

This book serves as an essential guide for individuals aiming to attain the Project Management Professional (PMP) certification, a globally recognized standard in project management. Its primary objective is to provide a thorough understanding of the comprehensive knowledge needed for the PMP exam, while also functioning as a career advancement tool by imparting crucial project management skills.

Uniquely, the book transcends the scope of just exam preparation. It dives deep into the principles of project management, emphasizing practical application in real-world situations. This ensures readers are not only exam-ready but also equipped with relevant, actionable insights for their professional life. The content aligns with the latest Project Management Body of Knowledge (PMBOK) Guide, guaranteeing up-to-date and applicable information.

Significantly, the book simplifies complex project management concepts, making them accessible to both beginners and experienced professionals. By including real-life examples, case studies, and practical exercises, it effectively bridges the gap between theory and practice, a critical element often missing in standard study materials.

The book also acknowledges the evolving nature of project management, incorporating contemporary methodologies like agile and hybrid approaches. This forward-looking perspective prepares readers for the future trends in the field, ensuring they are well-versed in both traditional and modern practices.

Moreover, the book acts as a catalyst for career development. It equips readers with a profound understanding of project management, laying a foundation for professional growth and success. It boosts confidence, empowering professionals to contribute significantly to their organizations and advance in their careers.

In conclusion, this book is an indispensable tool for PMP candidates. Its comprehensive approach, practical orientation, and adherence to current industry standards render it an invaluable resource for anyone aspiring to excel in project management.

Overview of PMP Certification: History and Evolution

The Project Management Professional (PMP) certification, developed by the Project Management Institute (PMI), has become a prominent and internationally respected credential in project management. Originating in the 1980s, the PMP certification marked a significant milestone in shaping the project management profession. It's now regarded as a standard of excellence, denoting proficiency and leadership in managing and directing projects.

PMP's evolution is a reflection of the maturation of project management as an independent professional discipline. Initially perceived as a component of other areas like engineering or construction, project management emerged as a distinct field due to the increasing complexity and essential role of projects in diverse industries. PMI introduced the PMP certification to validate the specialized skills and knowledge required in this evolving discipline.

Originally, the PMP certification primarily emphasized traditional project management approaches rooted in engineering and construction. These methodologies were appropriate for industries needing rigorous planning and control. However, as industries advanced and changes became more rapid, the domain of project management broadened to encompass more agile and flexible strategies, catering to the growing complexity of projects and the necessity for adaptable, responsive management.

A pivotal change in the PMP certification was the incorporation of agile and hybrid methodologies, aligning with the rising adoption of agile practices for projects demanding quick adaptability. This integration signified a comprehensive view of project management, recognizing project diversity across various sectors.

PMI has consistently updated the PMP certification to reflect the evolving landscape of project management. These updates include revisions to the PMBOK Guide, the cornerstone of the certification, introducing new processes, knowledge areas, and best practices in line with current trends and insights.

Recent updates to the PMP certification have placed greater emphasis on soft skills like leadership and communication, acknowledging that technical project management abilities must be balanced with strong interpersonal skills for effective team and stakeholder management.

The format of the PMP exam has also evolved, now featuring various question types to better evaluate a candidate's practical and theoretical knowledge in project management.

Overall, the PMP certification's development mirrors the dynamic nature of project management and its increasing significance in business. It highlights the necessity for project managers to continually adapt and enhance their skills, making the PMP certification not just an academic accolade but a crucial milestone in a project manager's career.

Target Audience and Best Practices for Using This Guide

This guide, meticulously designed for the PMP (Project Management Professional) certification, targets a diverse group of professionals aspiring to excel in project management. The primary audience includes individuals seeking to formalize and validate their project management skills through the globally recognized PMP certification. This encompasses a broad spectrum of professionals, ranging from novice project coordinators embarking on their project management journey to seasoned project managers aiming to solidify their expertise with a formal credential.

The book is particularly beneficial for professionals who have been involved in project initiation, planning, execution, monitoring, and closing, regardless of their industry. It caters to those in IT, construction, healthcare, energy, and government sectors, among others, recognizing that the principles of effective project management are universal across all domains. Additionally, the guide serves as an invaluable resource for team leaders and managers who, while not in formal project management roles, are involved in projects and seek to enhance their understanding and skills in this area.

For the best use of this guide, a few best practices are recommended:

1. **Structured Approach:** Begin by reading the introduction and the initial chapters to build a foundational understanding. Progress through the guide methodically, ensuring that each concept is thoroughly understood before moving to the next. This structured approach will reinforce learning and provide a comprehensive grasp of project management principles.

2. **Active Engagement:** Actively engage with the material. Utilize the practical examples, case studies, and exercises included in each chapter to apply the theoretical concepts in real-world scenarios. This active engagement aids in retaining information and understanding the practical application of project management techniques.

3. **Regular Revision:** Given the breadth and depth of the PMP exam content, regular revision is crucial. Revisit key concepts, terms, and methodologies periodically to ensure retention and understanding. Utilize the summaries and review questions at the end of each chapter to test your knowledge and identify areas that require further review.

4. **Collaborative Learning:** Where possible, engage with other PMP aspirants or professionals. Group discussions and study sessions can provide new insights, clarify doubts, and offer different perspectives on complex topics.

5. **Real-world Correlation:** Whenever possible, relate the concepts learned to your current or past project experiences. This correlation not only enhances understanding but also makes the learning process more engaging and relevant.

6. **Continuous Application:** Apply the learned principles in your current role or projects. Practical application of these concepts will reinforce learning and deepen your understanding of project management.

This guide, with its comprehensive coverage and practical orientation, is designed to be a valuable resource for PMP aspirants. By following these best practices, readers can maximize their learning and be well-prepared for both the PMP exam and their future roles in project management.

How This Book Differs from Other PMP Prep Materials

In a sea of resources for PMP (Project Management Professional) exam preparation, this book distinguishes itself through a unique blend of comprehensive coverage, practical application, and reader-centric approach. While there are numerous study guides and materials available, this book is crafted to provide a more holistic and engaging learning experience, setting it apart in several key ways.

1. **Balanced Theoretical and Practical Insights:** Unlike many prep materials that focus heavily on theory, this guide maintains a balance between theoretical knowledge and its practical application. It includes real-world scenarios, case studies, and practical examples that help readers understand how project management concepts are applied in various industries. This practical approach ensures that readers are not only preparing for the exam but also gaining skills applicable in their professional lives.

2. **In-Depth Topic Exploration**: While some materials skim the surface of complex topics, this book delves deepe, providing a thorough understanding of each subject. It goes beyond the PMBOK Guide, offering insights into the nuances of project management, which is crucial for a nuanced understanding required for the PMP exam.

3. **User-Friendly Structure and Language:** This guide is structured in a way that eases the reader into increasingly complex topics, making it suitable for individuals at various levels of their project management journey. The language used is formal yet accessible, avoiding overly technical jargon, which can be a barrier for readers new to the field.

4. **Focus on Recent Trends and Updates:** Recognizing the evolving nature of project management, this book includes the latest trends, methodologies, and best practices, including agile and hybrid approaches. It stays current with the most recent updates to the PMP exam and PMBOK Guide, ensuring readers have the most up-to-date information.

5. **Comprehensive Exam Preparation:** Beyond just covering the exam content, the book offers strategies for exam preparation, stress management, and effective study techniques. It includes a mock exam and a Q&A section, providing readers with an opportunity to test their knowledge in a format similar to the actual PMP exam.

In essence, this book is more than a study guide; it's a comprehensive, practical, and up-to-date companion for anyone aspiring to excel in the PMP exam and in the field of project management.

Why Your Support Matters for This Book:

Creating this book has been an unexpectedly tough journey, more so than even the most complex coding sessions. For the first time, I've faced the daunting challenge of writer's block. While I understand the subject matter, translating it into clear, logical, and engaging writing is another matter altogether.

Moreover, my choice to bypass traditional publishers has led me to embrace the role of an 'independent author.' This path has had its hurdles, yet my commitment to helping others remains strong.

This is why your feedback on Amazon would be incredibly valuable. Your thoughts and opinions not only matter greatly to me, but they also play a crucial role in spreading the word about this book. Here's what I suggest:

1. If you haven't done so already, scan the QR code at the beginning of the book to download the FREE SUPPLEMENTARY RESOURCES.

2. Scan the QR code below and quickly leave feedback on Amazon!

The optimal approach? Consider making a brief video to share your impressions of the book! If that's a bit much, don't worry at all. Just leaving a feedback and including a few photos of the book would be fantastic too!

Note: There's no obligation whatsoever, but it would be immensely valued!

I'm thrilled to embark on this journey with you. Are you prepared to delve in?
Enjoy your reading!

Study and Memorization Techniques.

Understanding the Material

Tackling the PMP exam requires more than just skimming through the PMBOK Guide and other resources. Truly understanding the material involves a deep and structured approach. In this subsection, we will explore some key techniques for approaching and understanding the core concepts for the PMP exam.

Creating a Study Structure

Before diving into studying, it's crucial to create a structure that guides your learning journey. Start by breaking down the material into manageable sections. For instance, you might divide the PMBOK Guide into knowledge areas or processes. This not only makes the material less overwhelming but also helps you focus on specific study areas at a time.

Active Reading Techniques

Apply active reading techniques. This includes highlighting, note-taking, and asking key questions while reading. Ask yourself: "How does this concept apply in the real world?" or "What is the rationale behind this practice?" This kind of questioning helps shift from passive memorization to active understanding.

Linking and Comparing

Look for connections between different concepts. Understanding how various knowledge areas and processes interact in the world of project management can help you better grasp the material. Comparing them to real-world project management experiences, even if they are simple projects you've managed in everyday life, can help make the material more tangible.

Discussion and Teaching

One of the most effective techniques is to discuss the concepts with others or try to teach them. Joining a study group or even explaining what you've learned to a friend can reveal new perspectives and solidify your understanding.

Utilizing Diverse Resources

Don't limit yourself to the PMBOK Guide. Leverage other resources like supplementary books, online forums, seminars, and webinars. Sometimes, a different explanation or a practical example can make a big difference in understanding a complex concept.

Summary

In conclusion, understanding the material for the PMP exam requires an active and involved approach. Creating a study structure, applying active reading techniques, making connections, discussing and teaching concepts, and using a variety of resources are all crucial steps for a solid understanding of the material. Remember, success in the PMP exam begins with deep understanding, not just surface-level memorization.

Memorization Techniques

Mastering memorization techniques is crucial for absorbing the vast amount of information required for the PMP exam. This section will delve into specific mnemonic methods tailored for PMP study, spaced repetition exercises, and the effective use of flashcards and diagrams.

Mnemonic Methods for PMP

Mnemonics are powerful tools for memorizing complex information, and they can be particularly effective for PMP study. One popular method is the use of acronyms. For instance, to remember the Project Management Process Groups, you can use the acronym "IPECC" - Initiating, Planning, Executing, Monitoring and Controlling, and Closing.

Another method is the creation of memory palaces. This involves associating the information you need to remember with specific locations in a familiar place, like your home. As you 'walk' through this space in your mind, you recall the associated information. For example, associating different knowledge areas of the PMBOK with different rooms in your house.

Spaced Repetition Exercises

Spaced repetition is a learning technique that involves increasing intervals of time between subsequent reviews of previously learned material. This method is highly effective for long-term retention of information. You can apply this technique using physical flashcards or digital tools like Anki or Quizlet, which have built-in algorithms to manage the spacing of repetition based on your performance.

To use spaced repetition for PMP study, begin by creating flashcards for key concepts, formulas, and processes. Each time you review the cards and successfully recall a concept, increase the time before you review that card again. If you struggle with a card, decrease the time interval. Over time, this method builds a robust long-term memory of the material.

Utilizing Flashcards and Diagrams

Flashcards are a classic and versatile tool for memorization. For PMP study, use flashcards to memorize formulas, definitions, and processes. On one side of the card, write a question or a keyword, and on the other side, write the answer or explanation. This method engages active recall, which is far more effective than passive review.

Diagrams, on the other hand, are excellent for visual learners. Creating flowcharts or mind maps of processes, frameworks, or the integration between different knowledge areas can help in visualizing and memorizing the information. For instance, drawing a diagram that shows the flow of processes across the knowledge areas can provide a visual representation that is easier to recall than text-based information.

Practice and Application

The key to effective memorization is consistent practice and application. Regularly test yourself on the material you have studied. This could be through practice exams, teaching the material to someone else, or even just verbally explaining a concept or a process.

Combining Techniques for Enhanced Learning

No single technique works best for everyone, so it's beneficial to combine these methods. Use mnemonics to get an initial grasp of complex information, spaced repetition to build and maintain your memory over time, flashcards for quick reviews, and diagrams for visual reinforcement. This multi-faceted approach caters to different learning styles and maximizes retention.

In conclusion, employing these memorization techniques can significantly enhance your ability to retain and recall the vast amount of information required for the PMP exam. Mnemonics help in initial memorization, spaced repetition ensures long-term retention, while flashcards and diagrams offer quick and visual ways to reinforce learning. Consistent practice and application of these methods will build a strong foundation for your PMP exam preparation.

Study Strategies

Developing effective study strategies is a cornerstone of successful preparation for the PMP exam. This section focuses on organizing study time, differentiating between active and passive study techniques, and the crucial role of breaks and stress management in your study regimen.

Organizing Study Time

Effective time management is essential for maximizing study efficiency, especially for a comprehensive exam like the PMP. Begin by creating a study schedule that aligns with your daily routine. Allocate specific time slots for PMP study, ensuring they are during periods when you are most alert and focused. Break down the PMP content into smaller, manageable segments and assign them to these slots.

Using tools like digital calendars or planners can help you track your progress and stay committed to your schedule. Remember, consistency is key, so try to stick to your designated study times as closely as possible.

Active vs. Passive Study Techniques

Understanding the difference between active and passive study techniques can significantly impact the effectiveness of your study sessions.

1. Passive Studying: This involves reading or re-reading notes, textbooks, or watching videos without much interaction. While it's a common method, it's often less effective because it doesn't engage deep cognitive processes necessary for long-term retention.

2. Active Studying: In contrast, active studying requires engagement with the material. This includes practices like self-testing, applying concepts to different scenarios, and teaching the material to someone else. Active studying is more effective because it forces you to retrieve information from memory and apply it, enhancing retention and understanding.

   Incorporate a mix of both techniques in your study plan, but emphasize active methods to ensure deeper understanding and longer retention of the PMP material.

The Importance of Breaks and Stress Management

Regular breaks and stress management are crucial in maintaining mental sharpness and overall well-being during your PMP prep.

1. Breaks: Integrate short breaks into your study sessions using techniques like the Pomodoro Technique, where you study for 25 minutes and then take a 5-minute break. This approach helps maintain high levels of concentration and prevents burnout. During breaks, engage in activities that are relaxing or invigorating, such as a short walk, meditation, or a light snack.

2. Stress Management: Preparing for the PMP exam can be stressful, and it's important to manage this stress effectively. Techniques like mindfulness, yoga, and regular physical exercise can help reduce stress levels. Additionally, ensure you get adequate sleep, as it is critical for memory consolidation and cognitive function.

   Maintaining a healthy balance between study and relaxation is vital. Overloading yourself can lead to burnout, while insufficient study can lead to under-preparation. Find a balance that works for you and stick to it.

Long-Term Commitment and Flexibility

Studying for the PMP exam is a long-term commitment. Be prepared to adjust your strategies as you progress. If certain methods aren't working, don't hesitate to try new techniques. Flexibility in your approach can lead to more effective learning.

In summary, effective study strategies for the PMP exam involve a well-organized study schedule, a focus on active study techniques, regular breaks, and efficient stress management. Balancing these elements can lead to a more productive and less overwhelming study experience. Remember, the key to success is not just the hours you put in but how effectively you use them.

Conclusion

We began by emphasizing the importance of truly understanding the material. A structured approach, breaking the content into manageable segments and employing active reading techniques, is vital not just for exam success but for a deep comprehension of project management principles.

Next, we explored memorization techniques, highlighting the efficacy of mnemonic devices and the importance of spaced repetition exercises and flashcards for long-term retention. These methods ensure that the learned material is retained not just for the exam, but also for professional application.

The discussion on study strategies underlined the need for organizing study time, prioritizing active over passive studying, and the critical role of breaks and stress management. These strategies aim to ensure that learning is sustainable and mentally healthy.

We also examined practical applications through case studies, demonstrating how these techniques can be applied in real-life project management scenarios. This bridged the gap between theory and practice, showing how knowledge can be transformed into applicable skills.

As you approach the PMP exam, it's crucial to maintain the confidence built through these strategies. Remember, the exam tests not just memory but the ability to apply principles in complex project management situations.

Armed with techniques for active studying, memorization, time management, and stress management, you're not just prepared to pass the exam but to excel in it. Let these strategies guide you in becoming a proficient project manager.

In conclusion, the effort invested in preparing for the PMP exam contributes to your growth as a professional. The path is rigorous but fosters personal and professional development. Each study technique brings you closer to not just certification but to becoming a more knowledgeable and skilled professional.

The success in the PMP exam reflects both the journey and the destination. Embrace this journey with enthusiasm and perseverance, knowing that every great project manager began with learning and determination. Good luck, and may your journey to PMP certification be as enlightening as it is rewarding!

Chapter 1: Key Project Management Terms

Essential Principles in Project Management

Grasping the key principles and terminology is vital in project management. This section introduces these essential concepts, forming a base for more complex subjects. It's important for both those preparing for the PMP exam and active practitioners to comprehend these basic elements for successful project management and exam preparation.

A project is essentially a short-term venture aimed at producing a distinctive product, service, or outcome. Defined by a clear start and finish, it is typically bound by specific objectives, resources, or deadlines. Projects differ from regular operations due to their temporary nature and distinctiveness, combining resources, skills, and technologies to achieve a goal, which could range from building construction to new software development.

Project Management involves applying knowledge, skills, tools, and techniques to project tasks to fulfill project needs. It covers various activities like initiation, planning, execution, monitoring, controlling, and concluding the project. Effective project management is key to achieving project goals within set parameters like scope, time, quality, and budget.

A program is a collection of interconnected projects managed together to gain benefits not possible from managing them individually. Programs might also include related work outside the scope of the individual projects. This is particularly important when multiple projects are interrelated or share a strategic objective.

A portfolio is a collection of projects, programs, subsidiary portfolios, and operations managed as a group to achieve strategic objectives. In contrast to a program, a portfolio's components may not always be interconnected or directly related.

The Project Management Office (PMO) is an organizational structure that normalizes project-related governance processes and aids in sharing resources, methodologies, tools, and techniques. The PMO's role varies from providing project management support to directly managing a project.

Stakeholders include any individuals, groups, or organizations that might influence, be influenced by, or believe they are influenced by a project's decisions, activities, or outcomes. They are crucial to a project's success, and their needs and expectations need to be understood and managed.

The Project Lifecycle denotes the phases a project undergoes from start to finish. Typical phases include initiation, planning, execution, monitoring, controlling, and closing. Each phase has specific goals and a series of activities and processes to complete.

Project Management Process Groups are organized groupings of project management processes designed to meet particular project objectives. The five groups are Initiating, Planning, Executing, Monitoring and Controlling, and Closing. Each group involves several processes and follows the same sequence in every project.

Knowledge Areas, as outlined in the PMBOK Guide, are specialized fields within project management, including areas like integration, scope, schedule, cost, quality, resource, communication, risk, procurement, and stakeholder management. Each area has specific processes to be conducted.

The Triple Constraint, also known as the project management triangle, symbolizes the three primary constraints on any project: scope, time, and cost. These constraints are interlinked, with changes in one often affecting the others. Balancing these constraints is essential for successful project management.

Scope Management involves defining and managing what is and is not part of the project. Effective scope management ensures that the project includes all the necessary work (and only that) to complete it successfully.

Risk Management is about identifying, analyzing, and responding to project risks. It focuses on maximizing the likelihood and impact of positive events and minimizing those of adverse events to the project's objectives.

Understanding these core concepts forms a foundation for exploring more detailed and complex aspects of project management. Mastery of these terms and definitions is crucial not only for passing the PMP exam but also for practical application in managing real-world projects.

In-Depth Overview of the PMBOK Guide

The PMBOK (Project Management Body of Knowledge) Guide, authored by the Project Management Institute (PMI), stands as a cornerstone in project management. Essential for those seeking PMP (Project Management Professional) certification, this guide delivers an exhaustive framework detailing standard terminologies, guidelines, and methodologies pivotal for proficient project management.

1. The PMBOK Guide's Evolution: Initially published to standardize project management practices, the guide has been regularly updated to keep pace with the dynamic field of project management. These revisions reflect new trends, practices, and the increasing complexity of projects across various sectors. The guide's ongoing updates ensure it remains a dynamic, relevant resource in the field.

2. Structure and Composition: The PMBOK Guide is meticulously structured, beginning with foundational concepts and the context of project execution. It progresses to an extensive examination of the project manager's role, highlighting necessary skills and competencies for effective leadership.

3. Core Framework: Central to the guide are the process groups and knowledge areas. The process groups—Initiating, Planning, Executing, Monitoring and Controlling, and Closing—depict the project lifecycle. Each contains distinct processes, often interrelated and overlapping. The knowledge areas—Integration, Scope, Schedule, Cost, Quality, Resource, Communication, Risk, Procurement, and Stakeholder Management—encompass domain-specific processes defined by their inputs, techniques, and outcomes, offering a comprehensive blueprint for project management.

4. Incorporation of Agile and Hybrid Approaches: The latest versions of the guide integrate agile and hybrid methodologies, highlighting its adaptability and comprehensive coverage of contemporary project management methods. This expansion reflects the guide's commitment to encompassing diverse project types and management styles.

5. Ethics and Professionalism: The guide emphasizes ethics and professional conduct, providing guidelines for ethical decision-making and behavior, crucial for maintaining professionalism and integrity in project management.

6. Global Standard with Flexibility: Recognized globally, the PMBOK Guide is versatile, allowing customization to fit different project environments and organizational requirements. It provides guidelines rather than fixed steps, enabling project managers to adjust practices to their unique project contexts.

7. Role in PMP Exam Preparation: For PMP exam candidates, the PMBOK Guide is indispensable. The exam heavily relies on the concepts, processes, and best practices from the guide. Comprehensive understanding and application of the guide's contents are essential for exam success.

Overall, the PMBOK Guide transcends its role as a PMP exam study resource. It serves as an extensive manual for managing diverse projects, notable for its structured approach, integration of various methodologies, focus on ethical practices, and adaptability, making it an invaluable tool for both aspiring and experienced project managers.

Terminology Specific to PMP: In-depth Analysis

The Project Management Professional (PMP) certification, overseen by the Project Management Institute (PMI), is underpinned by a distinct set of terms that are integral to its approach. For those aiming for PMP certification, mastering this terminology is essential. It plays a vital role not just in preparing for the exam but also in real-world project management situations. Let's delve into a detailed examination of some of the crucial terminologies associated with the PMP certification.

Earned Value Management (EVM) is a strategic approach in project management, designed to objectively track and evaluate a project's performance and advancement. It effectively merges key elements such as scope, time, and budget to provide a thorough assessment of a project's status. Within EVM, essential terms such as Planned Value (PV), Earned Value (EV), Actual Cost (AC), Schedule Variance (SV), and Cost Variance (CV) are critical in offering a clear and quantifiable overview of a project's progress and financial health.

Critical Path Method (CPM) is a key technique in project management, primarily utilized for planning and organizing project tasks. It focuses on identifying the sequence of dependent activities that take the longest time to complete, from the beginning to the end of the project. This method is instrumental in calculating the total duration required for a project's completion.

The Work Breakdown Structure (WBS) is a methodical breakdown of the entire scope of work needed for the project team to achieve project goals and produce the necessary deliverables. It stands as a crucial project deliverable, effectively organizing the team's tasks into manageable segments.

1. Risk Register: A critical element in the risk management strategy, the risk register is a comprehensive document that lists all recognized risks. It encompasses detailed descriptions of each risk, their causes, likelihood, potential impact, and the planned responses to address these risks.

2. RACI Chart: Representing Responsible, Accountable, Consulted, and Informed, this chart is a matrix tool in project management. It's utilized for delineating roles and responsibilities, ensuring tasks are clearly divided and allocated.

3. Scope Creep: This concept describes the gradual and often unchecked expansion of a project's scope, occurring at any stage once the project has commenced. Handling scope creep effectively requires meticulous management of the project's boundaries, determining what is and isn't part of the project's scope.

4. Gantt Chart: This widely-used tool in project management is essential for planning tasks and monitoring project timelines. It offers a visual representation of start and end dates, along with an overview of project activities.

5. Agile Methodology: Integral to modern project management and increasingly featured in the PMBOK guide, Agile is a methodology primarily used in software development. It encompasses a series of principles where project requirements and solutions progress through the joint efforts of interdisciplinary teams.

6. Six Sigma: This approach encompasses a collection of methodologies and tools aimed at enhancing process efficiency. Its primary goal is to elevate the quality of output in manufacturing and business operations by pinpointing and eliminating defect sources and reducing process variability.

7. Stakeholder Engagement Plan: This strategy outlines the identification of all stakeholders, examines their degree of interest, participation, influence, and the effect they have on the project, and details approaches for effectively engaging with them.

8. Procurement Documents: Essential components of the procurement management process, these documents encompass items such as Requests for Information (RFI), Requests for Proposal (RFP), and Requests for Quote (RFQ). They play a vital role in obtaining products, services, or results needed for the project from external sources.

PMI's Code of Ethics and Professional Conduct: This set of guidelines is pivotal for ethical decision-making within the realm of project management. It highlights the importance of responsibility, respect, fairness, and honesty in professional conduct.

Understanding these terminologies is essential for effective communication and management within the context of PMP. They not only help in passing the PMP exam but also equip professionals with the language needed to navigate the complex world of project management efficiently.

Common Misconceptions and Clarifications in PM Terminology

In the intricate world of project management, certain terminologies are often misunderstood or misapplied. These misconceptions can lead to confusion, miscommunication, and inefficiencies in project execution. Clarifying these terms is crucial for aspiring Project Management Professionals (PMPs) and practitioners in the field. Here are some common misunderstandings and their clarifications:

1. Project Manager vs. Program Manager: It's often mistakenly believed that these roles are similar, but they have distinct responsibilities. A Project Manager is tasked with overseeing the details of executing an individual project, including its scope, timeline, budget, and quality. On the other hand, a Program

Manager is responsible for managing a collection of interrelated projects, ensuring they are in harmony with the broader objectives and strategies of the organization.

2. Agile as a Methodology vs. Agile as a Mindset: There's a common misconception that Agile is solely a collection of methodologies, such as Scrum or Kanban. However, Agile transcends these practices, representing a mindset or philosophy that emphasizes adaptability, teamwork, ongoing enhancement, and responsiveness to change. The various methodologies are, in fact, practical applications of this Agile mindset.

3. Risk vs. Issue: Often confused as being the same, these terms hold different meanings in project management. A risk refers to a possible event or situation that could positively or negatively impact a project's goals if it materializes. An issue, on the other hand, is an existing problem currently affecting the project and necessitates prompt resolution.

4. Quality Assurance vs. Quality Control: These terms, while frequently interchanged, have distinct roles in project management. Quality Assurance (QA) is a procedural approach aimed at preventing flaws by verifying the effectiveness and efficiency of the processes managing and producing deliverables. Conversely, Quality Control (QC) is focused on the product, employing testing and inspection methods to detect any defects in the project's outputs.

5. Work Breakdown Structure (WBS) vs. Project Schedule: There's a common misconception equating WBS with a project schedule. However, WBS is a deliverable-focused hierarchical breakdown of the tasks the project team needs to perform, organizing the work into manageable parts. In contrast, the project schedule is a chronological plan that details the sequence and timing of completing the WBS components.

6. Project Scope vs. Product Scope: Often confused, these two terms have distinct meanings. Project scope is all about the entirety of work necessary to finish a project, covering every activity linked to the project. On the other hand, product scope focuses specifically on the characteristics and functionalities of the product or service being developed.

7. Critical Path vs. Fast Tracking: These two concepts, though related to project timing, differ significantly. The Critical Path is the lengthiest succession of activities in a project that dictates the earliest completion time. Conversely, Fast Tracking is a strategy employed to reduce the overall project timeline by conducting tasks simultaneously that were initially scheduled to be done one after another.

Clarifying these terminologies is vital for effective communication and successful project management. A clear understanding of these terms ensures that PMP aspirants and practitioners are on the same page, leading to more efficient project execution and better outcomes.

Chapter 2: Process and the Role of the Project Manager

The Comprehensive Project Management Process

At the genesis of every project lies the initiation phase. This is where the vision of the project takes root, germinating from an idea into a feasible endeavor. In this phase, project managers work like architects, conceptualizing the project's purpose and potential impact. They engage with stakeholders to outline the project's objectives, scope, and significance, setting the foundation upon which the entire project will be built. The creation of a Project Charter, a document that formally authorizes the project, marks the culmination of this phase, embodying the project's essence and its path forward.

Following initiation is the planning phase, where the project begins to take a definitive shape. Think of this phase as the blueprint of a building; it's where strategies are formulated and paths are charted. Project managers, in this phase, delve into the minutiae – outlining tasks, scheduling timelines, allocating resources, and setting budget constraints. Planning also involves risk assessment, where potential pitfalls are identified and mitigation strategies are developed. This phase is not a one-time event but a continuous process, adapting and evolving as the project progresses.

The execution phase is where these plans are brought to life. It's a dynamic phase, full of action and implementation, akin to the construction phase of a building. Here, project managers orchestrate the harmony of various elements – people, processes, and resources – to ensure that the project's objectives are met. They maintain a vigilant eye on the project's progress, ensuring that the team's efforts align with the project plan. Execution is often the most visible phase of the project management process, where the fruits of planning and strategy are realized.

Running parallel to execution is the monitoring and controlling phase. This phase is akin to a feedback loop in a complex system, ensuring that the project stays on track and deviations are corrected. Project managers monitor key performance indicators, track project progress, manage changes, and ensure quality standards are met. This phase is critical in maintaining control over the project, ensuring that it adheres to its predefined path, adjusting course as necessary.

The final chapter in the project management process is the closing phase. This phase is about bringing a structured end to the project, ensuring all tasks are completed, and objectives are met. Project managers in this phase focus on administrative closure, releasing resources, obtaining stakeholder acceptance, and documenting lessons learned. The closing phase is a reflective period, providing an opportunity to evaluate the project's successes and shortcomings, insights that become invaluable for future projects.

Throughout these phases, the role of a project manager evolves – from a visionary in initiation to a strategist in planning, a conductor in execution, an analyst in monitoring and controlling, and finally, a historian in closing. Each phase of the project management process is interwoven, with decisions and actions in one phase influencing the others. This process is not just a sequence of steps but a fluid, adaptive journey, accommodating the unique challenges and opportunities each project presents.

In essence, the comprehensive project management process is a blend of art and science – art in its ability to envision and inspire, and science in its methods and discipline. It's a journey that requires foresight, adaptability, and a deep understanding of the intricate dance between different project elements. Mastering this process is essential for any project manager aiming to lead their projects to success in the ever-evolving landscape of modern business.

In-depth Role and Responsibilities of a Project Manager

The role of a Project Manager transcends the conventional boundaries of managing tasks and timelines; it's a multifaceted journey through the lifecycle of a project, characterized by a blend of leadership, strategic thinking, and meticulous execution. This exploration delves into the in-depth role and responsibilities of a Project Manager, unraveling the layers that constitute this pivotal position in the realm of project execution.

At the heart of the Project Manager's role lies the art of defining project goals and objectives. This initial step is akin to setting the compass for a voyage, ensuring every team member and stakeholder understands the destination and purpose. The Project Manager, in this phase, is a visionary, aligning the project's goals with the organization's strategic objectives, and setting the tone for the journey ahead. This vision-setting is not just about articulating goals; it's about instilling a sense of purpose and direction in the entire team.

Once the goals are set, the Project Manager steps into the realm of planning, a phase that demands a meticulous and strategic mindset. Here, the Project Manager crafts a comprehensive plan that serves as the project's roadmap. This plan covers the spectrum of project requirements – from timelines and resource allocation to risk management and communication strategies. The planning phase is an intricate dance of foreseeing potential challenges, devising contingency plans, and setting a realistic yet ambitious path to project completion.

As the project shifts into the execution phase, the Project Manager's role evolves into that of a maestro, orchestrating various elements of the project. This phase is about bringing the plan to life, managing teams, overseeing tasks, and ensuring that every piece of the project puzzle fits perfectly. The Project Manager ensures that resources are utilized efficiently, timelines are adhered to, and the project's standards and objectives are met. Execution is a dynamic and action-packed phase, requiring the Project Manager to be proactive, responsive, and adaptable.

Parallel to execution runs the critical process of monitoring and controlling. The Project Manager, in this phase, is akin to a navigator, constantly charting the project's course and making adjustments as needed. This involves tracking the project's progress, managing changes, and ensuring quality control. It's a balancing act – maintaining the project's momentum while ensuring that it stays aligned with its initial objectives and parameters.

The culmination of the Project Manager's journey is the project closure, a phase that marks the completion of the project. Here, the Project Manager ensures that all project objectives are met, and the deliverables are accepted by the stakeholders. But the role doesn't end with the mere completion of tasks; it extends to capturing lessons learned, conducting post-project evaluations, and ensuring that the knowledge gained from the project is documented and shared. This phase is reflective, providing insights that are crucial for the growth and development of the team and the organization.

Beyond these phases, the Project Manager's role is imbued with the responsibility of leading and motivating the team. This leadership transcends traditional management; it's about inspiring the team, fostering a collaborative environment, and building a culture of accountability and excellence. The Project Manager navigates through diverse team dynamics, manages conflicts, and cultivates a workspace where each team member can thrive and contribute effectively.

Effective communication is another cornerstone of the Project Manager's responsibilities. It's not just about conveying information; it's about ensuring clarity, building trust, and fostering an environment of open dialogue. The Project Manager serves as the communication hub, bridging gaps between various stakeholders, resolving misunderstandings, and ensuring that everyone is on the same page.

Stakeholder management is also a critical aspect of the Project Manager's role. This involves identifying and understanding the needs and expectations of each stakeholder, and managing these throughout the project lifecycle. The Project Manager navigates through differing interests and perspectives, ensuring that stakeholder engagement is constructive and aligns with the project's objectives.

Quality management, an integral part of the Project Manager's responsibilities, involves ensuring that the project's deliverables meet the predefined standards. This is not just about adhering to technical specifications; it's about delivering value, ensuring customer satisfaction, and upholding the project's integrity.

Furthermore, the Project Manager's role extends to managing the project's budget and costs. This financial stewardship involves estimating costs, controlling expenditures, and ensuring that the project delivers value within its financial constraints. This aspect of the role requires a blend of analytical skills and financial acumen.

Risk management, another pivotal area, involves identifying potential risks, assessing their impact, and developing strategies to mitigate them. The Project Manager must be vigilant, proactive, and ready to respond to unforeseen challenges, turning potential obstacles into opportunities for growth and learning.

Essential Skills for Project Managers: A Comprehensive Guide

The role of a project manager transcends the mere orchestration of tasks and deadlines. It embodies a blend of diverse skills that range from technical acumen to emotional intelligence. The essential skills required for a project manager are like the colors on a painter's palette – each unique, yet when combined, they create a comprehensive picture of effective project management.

At the forefront of these skills is leadership – a quality that goes beyond mere management. A project manager, as a leader, doesn't just delegate tasks; they inspire and motivate their team. Leadership in project management is about setting a vision, navigating through challenges, and guiding the team towards the successful completion of the project. It involves creating a work environment where team members feel valued, empowered, and are motivated to contribute their best.

Communication is another skill that lies at the core of project management. A project manager's day is replete with communications – be it with team members, stakeholders, or clients. Effective communication in project management is multifaceted; it's not just about conveying information but also about listening, engaging in dialogue, and ensuring clarity and understanding. A project manager must be adept at adapting their communication style to various contexts and audiences, ensuring that their message is not just transmitted, but also received and understood.

Negotiation is a subtle art in the spectrum of a project manager's skills. It's not just about driving a hard bargain but more about finding a common ground where all parties feel their interests are addressed. Negotiation skills come into play in various scenarios, such as allocating resources, setting timelines, or managing scope changes. It requires a balance between assertiveness and empathy, understanding the other party's perspective while advocating for the project's needs.

Problem-solving and decision-making are like the twin stars guiding the project manager's journey. Projects, no matter how well planned, are often fraught with unforeseen challenges. A project manager must be able to think critically, assess situations, consider various solutions, and make informed decisions. This skill is not just about solving problems as they arise but also about anticipating potential issues and mitigating them proactively.

Time management is another vital skill in the project manager's repertoire. Managing a project is akin to juggling several balls simultaneously – each representing a different task or deadline. Effective time management is about prioritizing tasks, setting realistic deadlines, and ensuring that the project progresses on schedule. It also involves helping the team manage their time efficiently, ensuring that the workload is evenly distributed and manageable.

Technical project management knowledge forms the bedrock of the project manager's skill set. This encompasses an understanding of project management methodologies, processes, and best practices. A project manager should be well-versed in aspects like project lifecycle, risk management, budgeting, and quality control. Additionally, proficiency in project management tools and software enhances the efficiency and effectiveness of project planning and execution.

Team building and motivation are where the project manager's interpersonal skills shine. Building a cohesive and high-performing team is crucial for the success of any project. This involves not just assembling a group of skilled individuals but nurturing a team dynamic where collaboration and synergy are fostered. Motivating the team, especially during challenging times, is essential to maintain morale and productivity.

Adaptability and flexibility are the project manager's answer to the ever-changing project environment. Projects rarely go exactly as planned, and a project manager must be able to adapt to changing conditions and pivot strategies as needed. This flexibility is not just in response to external changes but also in adapting leadership and communication styles to suit the team's dynamic and project's context.

Emotional intelligence is an often-understated skill in project management. It's the ability to understand and manage one's emotions and to empathize with others. In the context of project management, emotional intelligence facilitates better relationships with team members and stakeholders, helps in navigating conflicts, and enhances the ability to lead with empathy and understanding.

Risk management, while a technical skill, also requires strategic foresight. It involves identifying potential risks, assessing their impact, and developing strategies to mitigate them. Effective risk management is not just about reacting to risks as they occur but about foreseeing potential challenges and planning for them in advance.

Customer focus is essential in today's project management landscape. A project manager must always keep the end-user or customer's needs at the forefront. This involves regular engagement with the customer, understanding their expectations, and ensuring that the project deliverables align with their requirements.

Business acumen, the ability to understand and apply business principles, is increasingly important for project managers. It involves understanding how the project fits into the larger organizational strategy and how it impacts the business. A project manager with strong business acumen can make more informed decisions, align the project more closely with business objectives, and contribute to the organization's success.

Lastly, continuous learning is what keeps a project manager relevant and effective. The world of project management is constantly evolving, with new methodologies, tools, and best practices. A commitment to lifelong learning ensures that a project manager remains at the forefront of the field, equipped with the latest knowledge and skills.

Evolution of Project Management Practices

The evolution is a fascinating journey through time, reflecting the changing needs and complexities of projects across eras. This evolution is not just a story of methodologies and tools; it's a narrative of how human ingenuity has adapted to the ever-changing landscape of organizational needs and technological advancements.

In the early days, project management was largely an unstructured process, often indistinguishable from general management. This was a time when projects, whether they were construction of monumental structures or large-scale manufacturing, were managed through basic principles of organization and command. The focus was primarily on getting the job done, often without specific methodologies or sophisticated tools.

The industrial revolution brought a shift in this approach. With the advent of complex engineering projects, there was a need for more systematic project management techniques. The late 19th and early 20th centuries saw the emergence of Gantt charts and the Critical Path Method (CPM). These tools introduced a more structured approach to project scheduling and resource allocation, providing project managers with a visual representation of project timelines and dependencies.

The mid-20th century marked a significant milestone in the evolution of project management. This era witnessed the formalization of project management as a distinct discipline. The establishment of the Project Management Institute (PMI) in 1969 and the subsequent introduction of standards like the Project Management Body of Knowledge (PMBOK) were indicative of this transition. The proliferation of large-scale, complex projects in sectors like aerospace, defense, and construction necessitated a more disciplined approach, leading to the development of various methodologies and frameworks.

The late 20th century saw the dawn of the digital age, which brought a paradigm shift in project management practices. The introduction of project management software revolutionized the way projects were planned, executed, and monitored. These tools enabled project managers to handle increasingly complex projects with greater efficiency and accuracy. The era was marked by a shift towards data-driven project management, where decision-making was increasingly based on data and analytics.

The turn of the millennium brought with it the Agile revolution. Originating in the software development industry, Agile methodologies emphasized flexibility, collaboration, and customer-centricity. The Agile Manifesto, published in 2001, challenged the traditional, plan-driven approach to project management and advocated for a more adaptive and iterative approach. Agile's emphasis on responding to change, rather than following a set plan, resonated with industries beyond software development, leading to its widespread adoption.

In recent years, the project management landscape has continued to evolve, embracing a more holistic approach. The recognition that different projects require different methodologies led to the rise of hybrid project management approaches. These approaches blend the predictability of traditional methods with the flexibility of Agile, providing a more balanced framework that can adapt to a variety of project types.

Additionally, the growing importance of soft skills in project management has become increasingly apparent. Emotional intelligence, leadership, and communication skills are now considered as crucial as technical project management skills. This shift reflects a broader understanding that successful project management is not just about managing tasks and schedules; it's about leading teams, managing stakeholders, and navigating the complexities of human dynamics.

The future of project management is likely to be shaped by further technological advancements, such as artificial intelligence and machine learning. These technologies promise to bring even greater efficiency and insights into project planning and execution. Additionally, the focus on sustainability and social responsibility is set to increase, as organizations recognize the importance of managing projects in a way that is environmentally and socially sustainable.

Process and the Role of the Project Manager Questions

1. What is the primary purpose of the initiation phase in project management?
2. Describe the role of a project manager during the planning phase.
3. How does the execution phase differ from the planning phase in project management?
4. What is the significance of the monitoring and controlling phase in project management?
5. Explain the role of a project manager in the closing phase.
6. How does the role of a project manager evolve throughout the different phases of a project?
7. What are two essential skills mentioned for project managers, and why are they important?
8. How have project management practices evolved from the industrial revolution to the present?
9. Describe the importance of risk management in the role of a project manager.
10. Why is continuous learning important for a project manager?

Process and the Role of the Project Manager Answers

1. Answer: The initiation phase is where the project's vision is established. It involves conceptualizing the project's purpose and impact, and engaging with stakeholders to outline objectives, scope, and significance. This phase sets the foundation for the entire project and is marked by the creation of the Project Charter.

2. Answer: In the planning phase, the project manager formulates strategies, outlines tasks, schedules timelines, allocates resources, and sets budget constraints. This phase also involves risk assessment, where potential pitfalls are identified, and mitigation strategies are developed.

3. Answer: The execution phase is where the plans formulated in the planning phase are put into action. It is a dynamic phase focused on implementation, where the project manager coordinates various elements – people, processes, and resources – to achieve the project's objectives.

4. Answer: This phase acts like a feedback loop, ensuring the project stays on track and deviations are corrected. It involves monitoring key performance indicators, managing changes, and ensuring quality standards are met. This phase is critical for maintaining control over the project and adjusting course as necessary.

5. Answer: In the closing phase, the project manager focuses on bringing a structured end to the project, ensuring all tasks are completed and objectives met. This includes administrative closure, releasing resources, obtaining stakeholder acceptance, and documenting lessons learned. It is a reflective period for evaluating the project's successes and shortcomings.

6. Answer: The project manager's role evolves from a visionary in the initiation phase to a strategist in planning, a conductor in execution, an analyst in monitoring and controlling, and finally, a historian in closing. Each phase demands different skills and approaches from the project manager.

7. Answer: Leadership and communication are two essential skills. Leadership is crucial for setting a vision, guiding the team, and navigating challenges. Communication is key for ensuring clarity, building trust, and fostering an environment of open dialogue.

8. Answer: Project management has evolved from basic organizational principles to structured methodologies like Gantt charts and the Critical Path Method. It further evolved with the establishment of formal standards like PMBOK, the introduction of project management software, and the Agile revolution. Today, it encompasses a blend of traditional and Agile methods, emphasizing technical and soft skills.

9. Answer: Risk management involves identifying potential risks, assessing their impact, and developing strategies to mitigate them. It is essential for a project manager to be proactive in foreseeing and planning for potential challenges, turning obstacles into opportunities for growth and learning.

10. Answer: Continuous learning is vital to stay relevant and effective in the field of project management, which is constantly evolving with new methodologies, tools, and best practices. It ensures that a project manager remains equipped with the latest knowledge and skills to lead projects successfully.

Chapter 3: Agile and Hybrid Project Management

Comprehensive Introduction to Agile Methodology

Agile methodology, a paradigm shift in the world of project management, has transcended its software development origins to become a vital approach in various industries. This methodology, distinguished by its adaptability and iterative nature, is a response to the fast-paced and constantly evolving business environment. Understanding Agile requires delving into its foundational principles, the philosophy behind its practices, and the impact it has on project management.

Agile emerged from the software development industry, where traditional project management approaches often struggled to keep up with the rapid pace of technological change. The Agile Manifesto, formulated in 2001 by a group of forward-thinking software developers, laid the groundwork for this approach. It emphasized flexibility, customer satisfaction, and the ability to adapt to change, challenging the rigid, linear processes of traditional methodologies.

The essence of Agile lies in its iterative approach to project delivery. Unlike traditional methods that aim to deliver a final product in one go, Agile breaks down the project into manageable units, allowing for regular reassessment and adaptation. This iterative process is not just about incremental development; it's about creating a rhythm of continuous improvement and responsiveness to change. It's a dance between planning and execution, where feedback is not an interruption but a vital input for the next step.

Agile is characterized by its emphasis on collaboration and customer involvement. The traditional model of handing down specifications from business to development teams is replaced by ongoing collaboration. In Agile, the customer is an integral part of the team, providing continuous input and ensuring the final product aligns with their needs and expectations. This collaborative spirit extends to the project team as well. Agile teams are self-organizing and cross-functional, blending various skills and perspectives to enhance problem-solving and innovation.

One of the key aspects of Agile is its focus on delivering value early and often. The approach prioritizes the rapid delivery of high-value features, enabling the project to demonstrate progress and functionality early in the lifecycle. This early and frequent delivery model not only provides immediate value to the customer but also helps in mitigating risks by identifying and addressing issues early in the process.

Adapting to Agile methodology also means embracing a culture of openness and flexibility. It requires a shift from a mindset of 'following the plan' to one of 'adapting to change.' This cultural shift is often the most challenging aspect of implementing Agile, as it involves changing long-standing practices and mindsets. Teams must learn to embrace uncertainty, use it as a tool for learning, and view change not as a threat but as an opportunity.

In Agile, feedback loops are a critical component. Regular reviews and retrospectives are not mere formalities; they are opportunities for honest reflection, learning, and adjustment. These feedback loops ensure that the project is continuously aligned with the customer's needs and the team is constantly improving its processes and practices.

Agile's impact on project management extends beyond methodologies and processes. It represents a more humane approach to project management, recognizing that teams are not just cogs in a machine but creative, dynamic individuals. Agile promotes a work environment that values people over processes, collaboration over silos, and adaptability over rigid planning.

Hybrid Approaches in Project Management: Theory and Application

The landscape of project management continually evolves, mirroring the dynamism of the business world. In this context, hybrid approaches in project management have emerged as a pivotal methodology, harmoniously blending the structured predictability of traditional models with the adaptive agility of contemporary practices. This nuanced amalgamation offers a versatile solution, tailored to navigate the multifaceted challenges of modern projects.

The genesis of hybrid project management is rooted in the recognition that no single approach can universally address the diverse spectrum of project requirements. Traditional methodologies, characterized by their sequential phases and emphasis on upfront planning, offer clarity and control but often lack the flexibility to adapt to change rapidly. Agile methodologies, in contrast, thrive on adaptability and iterative development but can sometimes fall short in providing a comprehensive roadmap for complex, multi-tiered projects. Hybrid project management emerges as a synergistic solution, marrying the best of both worlds to create a more holistic approach.

At its core, hybrid project management is an art of balance. It requires a deep understanding of the project's nature, objectives, and the environment in which it operates. This understanding is not static but evolves with the project, demanding constant reassessment and realignment. For instance, a project may commence with a traditional approach to establish a clear scope and deliverables, and then transition into Agile methodologies during the execution phase to benefit from iterative development and flexibility.

In practice, this fusion manifests in various forms depending on the project's demands. For a software development project, this could mean using Waterfall methodologies to outline the initial requirements and architecture, followed by employing Agile sprints for development and testing. In a construction project, the initial design and planning stages might follow a traditional approach, while the later stages of construction and finishing could incorporate Agile practices to better handle changes and unforeseen challenges.

This blended approach extends beyond methodologies to encompass mindset and culture. It necessitates an organizational culture that values flexibility, open communication, and collaboration. Project teams must be adept in both traditional and Agile practices, capable of shifting gears as the project progresses. This agility is not limited to processes but is ingrained in the way teams think, communicate, and make decisions.

Implementing hybrid project management also involves navigating the challenges that come with blending different methodologies. This includes managing stakeholder expectations accustomed to a particular approach, ensuring seamless communication across teams operating under different methodologies, and maintaining a cohesive project trajectory amidst varying practices.

Moreover, hybrid project management is not a static concept but a dynamic one, continuously evolving with each project's learnings. It is about drawing from experiences, refining practices, and developing a toolkit that can be customized for future projects. This evolutionary aspect is vital, as it ensures that the hybrid approach remains relevant and effective in the ever-changing landscape of project management.

Best Practices for Implementing Agile and Hybrid Methods in Projects

The adoption of Agile and Hybrid methodologies has become a cornerstone for success across various industries. However, the implementation of these methods is not merely about following a set of practices; it's about cultivating an environment conducive to their principles. This exploration delves into the best practices for effectively implementing Agile and Hybrid methods in projects, focusing on a narrative style to provide a cohesive understanding

The journey into Agile and Hybrid methodologies begins with a fundamental shift in mindset. Unlike traditional project management approaches that emphasize extensive planning and predictability, Agile is rooted in adaptability, collaboration, and customer-centricity. For a successful transition, organizations must embrace this cultural shift, moving away from rigid structures to a more flexible, responsive approach. This means redefining the way teams work, communicate, and deliver results.

Key to this transformation is the establishment of cross-functional teams. In Agile, teams are not just groups of individuals working together; they are cohesive units that embody the project's goals. These teams are empowered to make decisions, encouraging ownership and accountability. This empowerment is not merely about delegating tasks; it's about entrusting teams with the autonomy to find the best paths to project objectives. In this setting, the role of the project manager transforms from a director to a facilitator, guiding and supporting teams rather than dictating every move.

Communication holds a special place in Agile and Hybrid methodologies. It is not just frequent but also transparent and open, fostering a collaborative environment. Regular stand-ups, sprint reviews, and retrospectives are not mere formalities but platforms for honest dialogue and continuous improvement. These interactions go beyond status updates; they are opportunities for team members to align on goals, share insights, and collectively navigate challenges.

Adopting Agile and Hybrid methods also means embracing continuous learning and improvement. The iterative nature of these methodologies is not just about developing products in cycles but also about learning from each iteration. This learning is not confined to project teams; it extends to stakeholders and customers, involving them in the process. Feedback loops are integral, enabling teams to adapt and refine their strategies and deliverables in real-time.

One of the unique aspects of implementing Hybrid methodologies is the ability to blend the predictability of traditional methods with the flexibility of Agile. This blending, however, requires a nuanced understanding of the project's nature and objectives. It is about identifying which aspects of the project would benefit from a structured approach and which require agility. For instance, upfront planning might set the project's direction, but iterative development allows for navigating complexities and uncertainties as they arise.

Risk management in Agile and Hybrid environments takes on a proactive approach. Risks are not just identified and logged; they are continuously monitored and addressed as part of the iterative process. This approach enables teams to respond to risks promptly, often turning challenges into opportunities for innovation.

Moreover, implementing these methodologies is not a one-time effort but a continuous journey. It requires patience, persistence, and a willingness to evolve. Organizations must be prepared for a period of adjustment, where learning from setbacks is as important as celebrating successes. This journey is not just about achieving project goals but also about building a resilient, adaptive organization capable of thriving in a dynamic business landscape.

In essence, the successful implementation of Agile and Hybrid methodologies in projects transcends mere adherence to practices. It is about fostering a culture of flexibility, collaboration, and continuous improvement. It involves reimagining roles, redefining communication, and rethinking risk management. This shift is not just beneficial for individual projects; it positions organizations to be more responsive, innovative, and aligned with the evolving needs of their customers and markets. For Project Management Professionals, navigating this shift is not just a task; it is an opportunity to drive meaningful change and sustainable growth.

Case Studies: Agile and Hybrid Project Success Stories

Agile and Hybrid methodologies have proven their worth, not just as theoretical models but as practical approaches that drive real-world success. The stories of their implementation and outcomes offer valuable insights into how these methodologies can transform project execution and delivery. Let's explore some success stories that highlight the effectiveness of Agile and Hybrid methods in diverse scenarios.

1. In the software industry, a prominent technology firm experienced significant challenges in their product development cycle. Originally committed to conventional methodologies, they encountered extensive delays and an inability to effectively integrate customer feedback. This inefficiency necessitated a strategic shift towards Agile methodologies, a decision that proved transformative for their project management approach.

    Adopting Agile, the company restructured their development process into smaller, more manageable sprints. This segmentation allowed for more frequent reassessments and adjustments, fostering a dynamic workflow that could rapidly accommodate changes and new requirements. The inclusion of regular feedback loops was another critical aspect of their Agile implementation. These loops enabled continuous communication with customers, ensuring that the development trajectory remained aligned with user needs and expectations.

    This shift to Agile proved to be immensely beneficial. The company observed a marked acceleration in their development timeline, which was a direct consequence of the iterative sprint approach. Each sprint delivered a component of the product, allowing for quick iterations based on real-time feedback. This iterative process not only expedited the development but also significantly improved the product's relevance and quality. By aligning the product more closely with customer preferences and requirements, the team was able to deliver a solution that truly resonated with the market.

    Moreover, the transition to Agile had a positive impact on the team's morale. The developers and project managers, who were previously bogged down by the slower, more rigid traditional methods, found new enthusiasm in their work. The shorter development cycles of Agile sprints provided them with a sense of progress and achievement, as they could witness the tangible outcomes of their efforts more frequently. This boost in morale not only improved productivity but also fostered a more collaborative and innovative team environment.

    In conclusion, the company's adoption of Agile methodologies revolutionized their approach to product development. It enabled them to overcome the limitations of traditional project management, resulting in faster development times, higher product quality, and improved team dynamics. This case exemplifies the transformative power of Agile, highlighting its effectiveness in responding to customer needs, enhancing team morale, and accelerating product development in the competitive software industry.

2. In the banking sector, a significant success story unfolded at a large financial institution aiming to enhance its digital services. Initially, the project was structured around a traditional approach, characterized by meticulous upfront planning and a stringent execution strategy. This approach, while methodical, soon proved to be inadequate in the face of unexpected challenges and the dynamic nature of customer demands in the digital domain.

    As the project evolved, it became increasingly evident that the original plan lacked the necessary flexibility to adapt to the rapidly changing environment. Recognizing this, the institution made a strategic decision to shift to a Hybrid project management approach, effectively integrating Agile practices into their existing framework. This pivotal transition allowed the project team to respond more adeptly to the evolving landscape of digital banking services.

    The adoption of a Hybrid model facilitated a more iterative and responsive development process. By incorporating Agile methodologies, the team began to break the project into smaller, more manageable phases. This allowed for continuous evaluation and adjustment, ensuring that each stage of development was aligned with current user needs and market trends. Regular feedback loops became an integral part of the process, enabling the team to collect and implement real user feedback effectively. This approach was instrumental in creating a user-centered development environment, where customer insights directly influenced the evolution of the digital services.

    As a result, the digital platform underwent gradual yet consistent improvements. Each iteration brought enhancements and refinements, guided by actual user experiences and feedback. This iterative process not only ensured that the platform remained relevant and up-to-date but also significantly improved its usability and effectiveness. The end product was a digital service that was not only more user-friendly but also more aligned with the specific needs and expectations of the bank's customers.

    Moreover, this Hybrid approach had a broader impact on the institution's project management culture. It demonstrated the value of flexibility and adaptability in a sector traditionally dominated by rigid planning. The success of this project served as a catalyst for change within the organization, encouraging the adoption of more agile and responsive practices in other projects and initiatives.

    In conclusion, the financial institution's transition to a Hybrid project management approach was a key factor in the successful improvement of its digital services. By integrating Agile practices, the team was able to navigate the complexities of the digital banking landscape, responding effectively to unforeseen challenges and changing customer demands. This case study highlights the effectiveness of Hybrid methodologies in adapting to the fast-paced, customer-centric world of digital services, providing valuable insights for organizations in similar sectors.

3. In the healthcare sector, a compelling case study centers around a healthcare provider's endeavor to create a new patient management system. Initially, the project was structured with a well-defined framework, encompassing distinct stages and milestones, typical of traditional project management approaches. This method offered clear direction and a sense of order, which was initially considered beneficial for such a complex and sensitive project.

    However, as the project unfolded, it became evident that the rigid structure was insufficient to accommodate the evolving nature of healthcare requirements and patient needs. The complexity of integrating various healthcare processes and the critical necessity to address nuanced patient care demands called for a more flexible and responsive approach. To address these challenges, the project team pivoted to a hybrid approach, blending structured planning with Agile methodologies.

Incorporating Agile practices, such as iterative development and regular engagement with stakeholders, including healthcare professionals and patients, the team was able to adapt more effectively to the changing landscape of healthcare needs. This iterative process allowed for continuous refinement of the system, based on direct feedback and emerging insights. By engaging with end-users and stakeholders throughout the development process, the team gained valuable perspectives on patient care and administrative requirements, ensuring that the system's design and functionalities were closely aligned with real-world needs.

The hybrid approach facilitated the creation of a patient management system that was not only technically robust but also deeply attuned to the intricacies of patient care. The system's flexibility and adaptability made it capable of evolving with the changing dynamics of healthcare provision. This approach ultimately led to enhanced patient care, as the system was tailored to cater to specific patient needs and preferences. Additionally, it improved administrative efficiency by streamlining processes and incorporating feedback loops that allowed for ongoing improvements.

This case study in the healthcare sector highlights the efficacy of a hybrid project management approach, particularly in fields where projects are highly complex and involve sensitive, evolving requirements. By blending structured planning with the agility and user-centered focus of Agile practices, the project team was able to develop a solution that not only met technical specifications but also delivered significant value to end-users, demonstrating the transformative impact of adaptive project management in healthcare.

These stories exemplify the strengths of Agile and Hybrid methodologies. In the technology company's case, Agile's iterative nature and focus on customer feedback were key to accelerating product development and improving quality. In the banking project, the flexibility of the Hybrid approach allowed the team to adapt to a changing environment and user needs, resulting in a more effective digital service. And in the healthcare scenario, the combination of structured planning with Agile's adaptability led to a patient management system that was technically robust and user-centric.

In conclusion, Agile and Hybrid methodologies are more than just project management techniques; they are catalysts for innovation, efficiency, and alignment with customer needs. These success stories across various industries underscore the versatility and effectiveness of these approaches, demonstrating how they can be tailored to meet the unique challenges and requirements of different projects. By embracing the principles of Agile and Hybrid methodologies, teams can achieve not only project success but also drive broader organizational and industry advancements.

Agile and Hybrid Project Management Questions

1. What is the primary philosophy behind Agile methodology in project management?
2. How did the Agile Manifesto, formulated in 2001, influence Agile methodology?
3. Describe the iterative approach of Agile methodology in project management.
4. How does Agile methodology emphasize the role of customer involvement in project management?
5. What is the significance of delivering value early and often in Agile methodology?
6. Explain the cultural shift required for adopting Agile methodology in an organization.

7. What role do feedback loops play in Agile project management?
8. Define hybrid project management and its significance.
9. How does hybrid project management blend traditional and Agile methodologies?
10. What are the challenges involved in implementing hybrid project management?

Agile and Hybrid Project Management Answers

1. Answer: Agile methodology is fundamentally about embracing change and delivering value quickly. It breaks from traditional, linear project management approaches, focusing instead on adaptability, collaboration, and customer feedback. Agile prioritizes working solutions over extensive documentation and values human interactions over rigid processes. This philosophy is rooted in the belief that the best outcomes arise from responsive, iterative work cycles, and direct, ongoing collaboration with clients.

2. Answer: The Agile Manifesto, created by a group of software developers, laid the foundational principles of Agile methodology. It emphasized individuals and interactions over processes and tools, working software over comprehensive documentation, customer collaboration over contract negotiation, and responding to change over following a plan. This manifesto shifted the focus from a rigid, plan-driven approach to a more flexible, iterative approach that better accommodates the dynamic nature of modern projects, particularly in software development.

3. Answer: Agile's iterative approach divides projects into small, manageable segments, known as iterations or sprints. Each iteration involves planning, development, testing, and reviewing in short cycles. This approach allows teams to produce tangible results quickly and frequently, making adjustments based on regular feedback. It contrasts with traditional methods that aim for a single, final deliverable, enabling Agile teams to adapt more swiftly to changes in project scope or client requirements.

4. Answer: Agile methodology places significant emphasis on customer involvement throughout the project lifecycle. Unlike traditional methods where customer interaction might occur primarily at the beginning and end of the project, Agile involves customers at every stage. Regular feedback sessions and reviews with customers ensure that the project aligns with their needs and expectations, allowing for adjustments and improvements in real-time. This continuous engagement helps in building a product that accurately meets user requirements.

5. Answer: In Agile, the focus on delivering value early and frequently is pivotal. By prioritizing high-value features and delivering them in short cycles, Agile teams can provide immediate benefits to the customer, even as the project is ongoing. This approach not only enhances customer satisfaction but also allows for early identification and resolution of issues, reducing risks and avoiding the late discovery of problems. It aligns the project more closely with the customer's evolving needs and reduces time to market for products.

6. Answer: Adopting Agile methodology involves a significant cultural shift within an organization. It requires moving from a mindset focused on strict adherence to plans and processes to one that values adaptability and openness to change. This shift involves embracing collaboration over silos, encouraging team autonomy and decision-making, and prioritizing direct, open lines of communication. It also means

accepting that change is a constant and necessary part of project development, viewing it as an opportunity for improvement rather than a disruption.

7. Answer: Feedback loops are integral to Agile project management. These loops, through regular reviews and retrospectives, provide continuous opportunities for evaluation and adaptation. Teams reflect on what's working and what isn't, and make necessary adjustments to processes, strategies, and the product itself. This ongoing feedback from both the team and the customer ensures that the project remains aligned with business goals and customer needs, fostering a culture of continuous improvement and agility.

8. Answer: Hybrid project management is a methodology that combines elements of traditional (waterfall) and Agile project management practices. This approach recognizes that the rigid structure of traditional methods and the flexibility of Agile can be beneficial in different aspects of a project. Hybrid project management is significant in its ability to provide a balanced approach, leveraging the strengths of both methodologies to meet the specific needs of a project, especially in complex environments where both stability and adaptability are required.

9. Answer: Hybrid project management blends traditional and Agile methodologies by using a structured approach for initial planning and scope definition (often associated with traditional methods), followed by an iterative, flexible approach for project execution (characteristic of Agile). For example, a project may begin with a detailed planning phase to establish scope and deliverables, and then employ Agile sprints for development and implementation. This allows for clear project definition and management of stakeholder expectations, while still maintaining the ability to adapt to changes and incorporate feedback throughout the execution phase.

10. Answer: Implementing hybrid project management involves several challenges. It requires balancing the structure and discipline of traditional methods with the flexibility and adaptability of Agile. One challenge is ensuring cohesive communication and understanding among team members who may be more familiar with one methodology over the other. Another is managing stakeholder expectations, particularly if they are accustomed to a specific methodology. Additionally, maintaining a coherent project trajectory while integrating different practices can be complex, requiring strong leadership and an in-depth understanding of both methodologies to effectively blend them.

Chapter 4: Integration Management

Detailed Overview of Integration Management

At its core, Integration Management is about making disparate parts work together seamlessly. It's akin to conducting an orchestra, where the project manager ensures that every section contributes to a harmonious performance. In the context of a project, this means aligning various tasks, resources, and stakeholders' expectations to achieve the project's objectives. Integration Management is what transforms a collection of tasks and activities into a unified effort.

One of the primary challenges that Integration Management addresses is the inherent complexity of projects. Modern projects, often characterized by their multifaceted nature, require coordination across various domains. Whether it's aligning the project scope with customer expectations, balancing resource allocation, or synchronizing timelines, Integration Management is the thread that ties these aspects together. It ensures that decisions made in one area of the project are aligned with the goals and constraints of other areas, maintaining the project's overall integrity.

A key aspect of Integration Management is the development and upkeep of the project management plan. This plan is not just a document; it's a roadmap that guides the entire project. Crafting this plan requires a deep understanding of the project's objectives, resources, constraints, and risks. It involves integrating plans from different areas, such as scope, schedule, cost, quality, and resources, into a comprehensive guide that steers the project through its lifecycle.

Effective Integration Management also involves monitoring and controlling project work. This is where the project manager ensures that the project stays on course, making adjustments as necessary. It involves tracking the project's progress against the management plan, managing changes in a controlled manner, and ensuring that project objectives are being met. This continuous oversight is crucial, as it allows for timely identification and resolution of issues, minimizing their impact on the project.

Another critical element of Integration Management is managing project knowledge. This involves capturing, sharing, and utilizing knowledge gained throughout the project. It's about learning from each phase, each task, and applying this knowledge to improve processes and decision-making. Effective knowledge management not only enhances the current project but also provides valuable insights for future projects.

Integration Management also plays a crucial role during project closure. This phase involves bringing the project to an orderly end, ensuring that all objectives have been met, and that deliverables are accepted by the stakeholders. It's about integrating all the final pieces – from completing remaining tasks to documenting lessons learned. The closure phase is an opportunity to reflect on the project's success, understand what worked well, and identify areas for improvement.

The role of the project manager in Integration Management is multifaceted. It requires a blend of technical skills, strategic thinking, and leadership qualities. The project manager must be adept at understanding the big picture while also paying attention to the details. They need to be effective communicators, capable of conveying the project's vision and aligning the team and stakeholders towards common goals. They also need to be flexible, able to adapt to changes and guide the project through challenges and uncertainties.

Integration Management is a critical discipline in project management, providing the glue that binds together all aspects of a project. It involves a strategic approach to combining and coordinating individual project elements, ensuring that they work together effectively to achieve the project's objectives. Through effective Integration Management, a project manager can navigate the complexities of modern projects, delivering results that meet or exceed stakeholders' expectations. This discipline is not just about managing tasks; it's about creating synergy, where the sum of the project's parts creates a greater, more successful whole.

Processes in Developing Project Charter and Management Plan

The Project Charter marks the birth of the project. It's the formal authorization that breathes life into the project, giving the project manager the authority to use organizational resources and lead the project. The creation of the Project Charter is like laying the cornerstone of a building. It involves identifying the purpose of the project, its objectives, and the roles and responsibilities of the project team. This document is a product of collaborative efforts, drawing inputs from key stakeholders, sponsors, and experts. It's a high-level document that outlines the project's vision, scope, and boundaries. The Charter provides a clear direction and a sense of purpose, not just for the project manager but for the entire team.

Developing the Project Charter begins with understanding the needs and expectations of the stakeholders. This involves discussions, meetings, and negotiations, ensuring that the project's objectives align with the organization's strategic goals. It's a process that requires the project manager to have a strong grasp of business needs, a keen sense of negotiation, and the ability to balance different perspectives and interests.

The Project Charter also sets out the initial requirements for the project. This includes a preliminary definition of the project's scope, highlighting what will be included and what will be excluded from the project. It also outlines the key deliverables, the high-level timeline, and the major constraints and assumptions that will guide the project. The Charter serves as a reference point throughout the project, helping to keep the project aligned with its initial goals and objectives.

Once the Project Charter is established, the focus shifts to the development of the Project Management Plan. This plan is the blueprint of the project; it's a comprehensive document that details how the project will be executed, monitored, and controlled. Developing the Project Management Plan is a meticulous process, involving in-depth planning and coordination across various aspects of the project.

The process of creating the Project Management Plan is iterative and collaborative. It involves deep dives into each aspect of the project, from scope management and schedule planning to cost estimation and quality management. The plan is a detailed map that guides the project team through the execution of the project. It lays out the methodologies to be used, the resources required, and the management strategies that will be applied. It also includes detailed plans for how risks will be managed, how communication will be handled, and how stakeholders will be engaged.

In developing the Project Management Plan, the project manager acts as a conductor, harmonizing inputs from team members, stakeholders, and subject matter experts. This process requires a high level of expertise in project management methodologies, as well as strong communication and facilitation skills. The project manager needs to ensure that the plan is comprehensive yet flexible, detailed yet adaptable.

The Project Management Plan also outlines the metrics and key performance indicators that will be used to measure the project's progress. It includes mechanisms for tracking performance, monitoring risks, and managing changes. This plan is not static; it evolves as the project progresses, adapting to changes and new insights.

Both the Project Charter and the Project Management Plan are crucial in setting the foundation for a successful project. The development of these documents is a complex process that requires strategic thinking, collaborative efforts, and meticulous planning. They provide a framework for the project, ensuring that it is well-defined, well-planned, and aligned with the organization's goals.

The processes of developing the Project Charter and the Project Management Plan are fundamental to the success of any project. These documents serve as guiding lights, providing direction and structure to the project. They require a blend of strategic vision, collaborative input, and detailed planning, ensuring that the project is set up for success from the very beginning. For the project manager, these processes are not just about creating documents; they are about laying the groundwork for a successful journey from project inception to completion.

Advanced Techniques in Directing, Managing, Monitoring, and Controlling Project Work

The complexities of directing, managing, monitoring, and controlling project work is akin to conducting a symphony orchestra. Each musician plays a critical part, and the conductor must ensure harmony and synchrony to create a melodious performance. In project management, this translates into a blend of strategic oversight, proactive management, and continuous refinement, ensuring the project stays on course and achieves its objectives.

At the heart of directing and managing project work lies a nuanced understanding of the project's goals and a clear vision of how to achieve them. This process starts with a detailed project management plan, but it extends far beyond that. The project manager must be adept at translating this plan into actionable tasks, effectively allocating resources, and ensuring the team's efforts are aligned with the project's objectives. It involves not just assigning roles and responsibilities but also motivating and inspiring the team to perform at their best.

Advanced project management often employs adaptive leadership styles. The project manager tailors their approach to the needs of the team and the nature of the project. In some instances, a more directive approach is necessary, especially when dealing with critical decisions or risks. In other situations, a collaborative style fosters creativity and innovation. This adaptability in leadership is crucial in navigating the diverse challenges and dynamics that projects typically encounter.

Monitoring and controlling project work is a continuous process that ensures the project stays aligned with its plan. It involves tracking the project's progress against its objectives, assessing performance, and implementing changes where necessary. Advanced techniques in this domain often include the use of sophisticated project management software and tools. These tools provide real-time data and analytics, enabling the project manager to make informed decisions based on current project status and trends.

Risk management plays a pivotal role in the monitoring and controlling phase. Advanced risk management involves not just identifying potential risks but also continuously assessing these risks throughout the project lifecycle. This proactive approach enables the project manager to anticipate problems before they occur and implement strategies to mitigate their impact. It involves a deep understanding of the project's environment and the ability to think critically about potential future scenarios.

Quality management is another critical aspect of project monitoring and control. It goes beyond ensuring that the project's deliverables meet certain standards; it's about embedding quality into every aspect of the project management process. This involves regular quality audits, reviews, and assessments, ensuring that the project's processes and outputs consistently meet the defined quality criteria.

Communication is the thread that ties together all aspects of directing, managing, monitoring, and controlling project work. Advanced project management recognizes the importance of effective communication – not just in disseminating information but in fostering an environment of openness and transparency. It involves regular and clear communication with the team, stakeholders, and clients, ensuring that everyone is informed and engaged throughout the project's lifecycle.

Change management is an integral part of advanced project management techniques. Projects often encounter changes, whether in scope, timelines, or resources. Managing these changes effectively involves assessing the impact of the change, communicating it to all relevant parties, and adjusting the project plan accordingly. It requires a balance between flexibility and control, ensuring that changes are managed in a way that benefits the project while maintaining its objectives.

The advanced techniques in directing, managing, monitoring, and controlling project work are about much more than just following a plan. They involve a dynamic interplay of strategic decision-making, adaptive leadership, sophisticated tools and techniques, and continuous improvement. The project manager, in this context, is not just an overseer but an orchestrator, guiding the project through its various phases, adapting to challenges, and steering it towards success. This approach is not just about ensuring that the project meets its objectives; it's about creating a framework where excellence, innovation, and collaboration thrive, leading to outcomes that exceed expectations.

Integration Management Challenges and Solutions

A critical aspect of project management, involves cohesively blending various project elements to ensure a unified operation and successful outcome. However, this process is often fraught with challenges, each requiring strategic solutions to navigate effectively.

One primary challenge in Integration Management is maintaining a clear and consistent vision across the project's lifecycle. Projects, especially large and complex ones, can easily veer off course due to varying interpretations of objectives and goals. This situation is akin to a ship where every crew member has a different map; without a unified direction, reaching the destination becomes a challenge. The solution lies in establishing a clear and well-communicated vision from the outset. The project manager must articulate the project goals and objectives clearly and ensure that every team member understands and aligns with this vision. Regular meetings, clear communication channels, and documented goals can aid in maintaining this clarity.

Another significant challenge is managing the diverse and often conflicting interests of stakeholders. Each stakeholder comes with their own set of expectations, priorities, and requirements, which can complicate the integration process. To address this, effective stakeholder management is key. This involves identifying all stakeholders early in the project, understanding their needs and expectations, and managing them throughout the project. Regular communication, involving stakeholders in decision-making processes, and finding compromises where necessary can help in aligning their interests with the project objectives.

Integration Management also encounters the challenge of harmonizing different methodologies and processes used within the project. In today's diverse project environments, teams might employ various methodologies, such as Waterfall, Agile, or a hybrid of both. Aligning these different methodologies can be like trying to fit square pegs into round holes. The solution lies in adopting a flexible and adaptive approach. The project manager should understand the strengths and limitations of each methodology and find ways to integrate them seamlessly. This might involve customizing processes, encouraging cross-methodology understanding among team members, and finding a common ground that respects the principles of each approach.

Changes in project scope, timelines, and resources are another hurdle in Integration Management. Changes are inevitable in most projects, but if not managed properly, they can lead to scope creep, delays, and budget overruns. Effective change management processes are vital to tackle this challenge. This includes establishing clear procedures for handling changes, assessing the impact of each change, and ensuring transparent communication about the changes to all stakeholders. It also involves revisiting and adjusting the project plan as necessary to accommodate these changes.

Lastly, maintaining quality and consistency across the project can be challenging, especially when dealing with large teams and multiple workstreams. The solution is to implement rigorous quality control and assurance processes. This involves setting clear quality standards, conducting regular quality audits, and engaging in continuous process improvement. Quality should be an integral part of every phase of the project, from planning to execution.

Integration Management is a complex yet crucial aspect of project management, requiring a blend of strategic thinking, effective communication, and adaptive leadership. The challenges in this domain are diverse, ranging from maintaining a unified vision to managing changes and stakeholder interests. Addressing these challenges requires a combination of clear communication, stakeholder engagement, flexible methodology integration, effective change management, and rigorous quality control. By navigating these challenges effectively, a project manager can ensure that the various elements of the project are seamlessly integrated, leading to a successful and cohesive project outcome.

Integration Management Questions

1. What is the main purpose of Integration Management in project management?
2. How does Integration Management address the complexity of modern projects?
3. What is the significance of the project management plan in Integration Management?
4. What are the key responsibilities of a project manager in monitoring and controlling project work?
5. How does effective Integration Management contribute to project knowledge management?
6. Describe the role of Integration Management during the project closure phase.
7. What skills are essential for a project manager in the context of Integration Management?
8. How does the Project Charter contribute to the success of a project in Integration Management?
9. What processes are involved in developing the Project Management Plan?
10. What are some common challenges in Integration Management, and how can they be addressed?

Integration Management Answers

1. Answer: The primary purpose of Integration Management is to combine and coordinate various elements of a project to ensure they work together effectively, transforming a collection of tasks and activities into a unified effort.

2. Answer: Integration Management addresses the complexity of projects by ensuring coordination across various domains, aligning project scope with customer expectations, balancing resource allocation, and synchronizing timelines.

3. Answer: The project management plan is crucial as it acts as a comprehensive guide that steers the project through its lifecycle, integrating plans from different areas into a unified roadmap.

4. Answer: A project manager's responsibilities in monitoring and controlling project work include tracking progress against the management plan, managing changes in a controlled manner, and ensuring project objectives are met.

5. Answer: Effective Integration Management enhances project knowledge management by capturing, sharing, and utilizing knowledge gained throughout the project, thus improving processes and decision-making.

6. Answer: During project closure, Integration Management plays a crucial role in ensuring all objectives have been met, deliverables are accepted, and involves integrating final pieces like completing tasks and documenting lessons learned.

7. Answer: Essential skills for a project manager in Integration Management include technical expertise, strategic thinking, effective communication, flexibility, and leadership qualities.

8. Answer: The Project Charter is significant as it provides formal authorization for the project, outlines its vision, scope, and boundaries, and sets a clear direction and purpose for the entire team.

9. Answer: Developing the Project Management Plan involves in-depth planning and coordination across various aspects of the project, including scope, schedule, cost, and quality management, creating a detailed blueprint for project execution.

10. Answer: Common challenges in Integration Management include maintaining a unified project vision, managing diverse stakeholder interests, harmonizing different methodologies, managing changes, and maintaining quality. These can be addressed through clear communication, stakeholder engagement, flexible methodology integration, effective change management, and rigorous quality control processes.

Chapter 5: Project Scope Management

Advanced Understanding of Scope Management

In project management, Scope Management is essentially the process of delineating the exact boundaries of a project. It involves a clear definition of what is included in the project's scope and, crucially, what is excluded. This precise demarcation is vital for ensuring the project remains focused and on track, delivering exactly what is required without straying into superfluous areas that can dilute its effectiveness and efficiency.

At its heart, advanced Scope Management is about developing a clear and detailed understanding of the project's goals and deliverables. This clarity is not just a starting point but a continual reference throughout the project's life. It involves in-depth discussions with stakeholders, meticulous gathering of requirements, and a thorough understanding of the project's context. Imagine building a map that guides the project; Scope Management is about drawing the lines that define this map's edges, ensuring everyone involved knows the territory's extent.

However, defining the scope is only part of the challenge. The more intricate aspect is managing and controlling this scope throughout the project. Scope creep, a common phenomenon where the project's scope gradually expands beyond its initial boundaries, often unnoticed, can be a significant threat to the project's success. It's like a tide that slowly encroaches upon the shore; if not monitored and controlled, it can engulf the entire land.

Preventing scope creep requires a combination of vigilance and flexibility. It involves setting up robust processes for monitoring the project's progress and implementing change control mechanisms. Any request for changes in scope must be rigorously evaluated for its impact on the project's resources, timeline, and quality. This process is not just about saying no to additional requests; it's about assessing the value these changes bring to the project and making informed decisions that align with the project's objectives.

Effective communication plays a pivotal role in Scope Management. The project manager must ensure that all stakeholders have a shared understanding of the project's scope. This involves regular and transparent communication about the project's progress, any changes in scope, and their implications. It's a continuous process of ensuring alignment and managing expectations.

Another critical aspect of Scope Management is documentation. Comprehensive documentation of the project's scope, including the project scope statement, work breakdown structure, and detailed project plan, provides a clear reference for what has been agreed upon. This documentation is not static; it evolves as the project progresses, capturing any changes and decisions made along the way.

Advanced Scope Management also involves foreseeing potential scope-related issues and planning for them. This foresight can be developed through experience and a deep understanding of the project's environment. It involves anticipating where changes might occur, understanding the project's high-risk areas, and having contingency plans in place.

Advanced Scope Management is a dynamic and critical component of project management. It goes beyond simply defining what the project will deliver; it's about continually managing and safeguarding the project's scope. This process requires a mix of strategic planning, rigorous evaluation, clear communication, and thorough documentation. By mastering Scope Management, a project manager ensures that the project remains focused and aligned with its original objectives, delivering precisely what it was intended to, with optimal resources and within the desired timeline.

Processes for Detailed Planning and Controlling Project Scope

This process is akin to drawing a map for a journey; it outlines the path to be taken, landmarks to be reached, and boundaries not to be crossed. It's a delicate balance between the envisioned end result and the practical steps required to get there.

The scope management begins with an in-depth understanding of what the project aims to achieve. It starts with conversations, deep dives into the project's purpose, and the outcomes expected. This initial stage is where visions and ideas take a concrete form. The project manager acts as a bridge between the project's goals and the practical realities of achieving them. They navigate through various stakeholders' inputs, expectations, and constraints, weaving them into a unified and agreed-upon project scope.

Once the scope is defined, the next step is to detail it into a comprehensive plan. This plan is not just a list of tasks; it's a blueprint that articulates how the scope will be achieved. It involves breaking down the project scope into smaller, manageable components, a process known as creating the Work Breakdown Structure (WBS). The WBS is like a tree, with the project's main objectives as the trunk and the smaller tasks and deliverables as the branches and leaves. This breakdown makes it easier to assign responsibilities, allocate resources, and set timelines.

But detailing the plan is only part of the journey. The real challenge lies in adhering to this plan throughout the project's lifecycle, a task that requires constant vigilance and adaptability. Controlling the project scope is about ensuring that the project stays on track, aligned with the plan. It's about being the guardian of the project's boundaries, vigilant against scope creep – the subtle and often unnoticed expansion of the project's scope.

Controlling the scope involves continuously monitoring the project's progress and comparing it against the plan. This monitoring is not just a periodic check; it's an ongoing process of observation and analysis. The project manager must be alert to any deviations from the plan, whether they are slight detours or significant changes. They must assess the impact of these deviations and decide whether to incorporate them into the project scope or realign the project to its original path.

Managing changes to the project scope is another critical aspect. Changes are inevitable, and the project manager must have a robust process for handling them. This involves evaluating the change requests, understanding their impact on the project, and making informed decisions about whether to accept, reject, or modify these requests. It also involves updating the project plan and communicating these changes to all stakeholders, ensuring that everyone is aware of the new direction.

Throughout this process, communication plays a vital role. Clear, transparent, and regular communication ensures that all stakeholders are on the same page, understand the project's progress, and are aware of any changes in the scope. It's about keeping the lines of communication open, encouraging feedback, and fostering an environment of collaboration.

Detailed planning and controlling of a project's scope is a meticulous and dynamic process. It requires a deep understanding of the project's objectives, a strategic approach to planning, constant vigilance to stay on track, and an adaptive mindset to manage changes. It's a process that demands precision, foresight, and effective communication. By mastering these aspects of scope management, a project manager ensures that the project not only meets its objectives but does so efficiently, effectively, and with the support and agreement of all stakeholders.

Techniques for Defining and Managing Project and Product Scope

Defining and managing the scope of a project and its product is akin to charting a course for a ship, where every decision impacts the journey's success. The process is both an art and a science, requiring a blend of precision, foresight, and adaptability.

It's about understanding the project's purpose, the desired outcomes, and the boundaries within which the project must operate. This initial step is much like painting a picture; the project manager must capture the vision of the project in broad strokes, setting the stage for the finer details to be filled in later. Engaging with stakeholders, understanding their needs and expectations, and translating these into a coherent and achievable plan is crucial at this stage.

In parallel, defining the product scope is about detailing the characteristics and requirements of the product or service that the project will deliver. This process is more technical and requires a deep understanding of what the end users need and expect from the product. It's a meticulous task, akin to drafting the blueprint of a building, where every element must be carefully planned and articulated.

Once the scopes are defined, the next challenge is managing them throughout the lifecycle of the project. Managing project and product scope is not a static task but a dynamic process that requires constant attention and adaptation. It involves ensuring that the project stays aligned with the initial scope and that any deviations are carefully managed.

One key technique in managing scope is the use of a Work Breakdown Structure (WBS). The WBS breaks down the project into smaller, manageable parts, making it easier to monitor progress and manage changes. Think of it as a map that guides the project team; each section of the WBS is a landmark, helping to keep the project on its intended path.

Regular scope reviews are another vital technique. These reviews are not just checkpoints; they are opportunities to assess the project's progress, to ensure that it is still aligned with the initial scope, and to make adjustments as necessary. This process is much like navigating a ship; the project manager must regularly check their bearings and adjust the course as needed.

Change control is a critical aspect of scope management. In any project, changes are inevitable, but how they are managed can make the difference between success and failure. Implementing a robust change control process involves assessing the impact of each change, deciding whether it aligns with the project's goals, and determining how it will affect the project's timeline and resources. It's a delicate balancing act, requiring the project manager to weigh the benefits of the change against the risks it may pose to the project's success.

Communication plays a pivotal role in managing project and product scope. Keeping stakeholders informed about the project's progress, any changes in scope, and the reasons behind these changes is essential. Effective communication ensures that everyone involved has a clear understanding of the project's status and direction, reducing the risk of misunderstandings and conflicts.

Defining and managing project and product scope is a complex process that requires a strategic approach, attention to detail, and the ability to adapt to changes. It involves not just setting the boundaries of the project but also guiding it through the various challenges and changes that arise along the way. By mastering these techniques, a project manager can ensure that the project remains focused, aligned with its objectives, and adaptable to the evolving needs of stakeholders and the market. This process is key to delivering a product that meets the end users' needs and a project that achieves its goals efficiently and effectively.

Scope Creep: Prevention and Management

Scope creep is akin to an uninvited guest at a party, subtly arriving and gradually taking over. It refers to the insidious expansion of a project's scope without proper authorization or adjustments to time, cost, and resources. Managing scope creep is crucial, as it can derail a project, leading to budget overruns, delayed timelines, and unmet objectives.

The prevention and management of scope creep begin with a clear and comprehensive definition of the project's scope. Like a painter who sketches before applying color, the project manager must outline the project's boundaries and deliverables at the outset. This definition should be detailed, unambiguous, and aligned with the stakeholders' expectations and needs. It serves as a reference point throughout the project, a compass to guide decision-making and evaluate requests for changes.

Effective communication is paramount in preventing scope creep. It involves not just relaying information but ensuring that it is understood and acknowledged by all parties involved. Regular meetings, updates, and open lines of communication help in maintaining transparency and alignment. The project manager acts as a bridge, ensuring that everyone, from team members to stakeholders, is on the same page regarding the project's scope, goals, and progress.

However, even with the best initial planning, changes are inevitable. This is where robust change management processes come into play. These processes should be well-defined, structured, and integrated into the project management plan. Every request for change should be thoroughly evaluated for its impact on the project's scope, resources, timeline, and quality. The decision to incorporate a change should be weighed carefully, considering the project's overall objectives and constraints.

Monitoring and controlling the project's progress are crucial in managing scope creep. This involves keeping a vigilant eye on the project's trajectory, continuously comparing it against the initial plan. The project manager must be proactive, identifying deviations early, and addressing them before they escalate. Regular status reviews and progress reports are tools that aid in this monitoring, helping to ensure that the project remains on track.

Stakeholder management is also a critical component in preventing scope creep. Stakeholders, with their varying interests and perspectives, can often be sources of scope creep. Managing their expectations, addressing their concerns, and involving them in decision-making processes can help in minimizing unwarranted changes and requests. It's about striking a balance between accommodating stakeholders' needs and maintaining the project's integrity.

Lastly, the project manager's leadership and negotiation skills play a key role. They must be firm yet flexible, capable of saying no when necessary and negotiating compromises that align with the project's goals. This requires a deep understanding of the project's objectives, strong communication skills, and the ability to make decisions that balance the needs of all parties involved.

Preventing and managing scope creep is an ongoing process that requires vigilance, clear communication, robust change management, and proactive stakeholder engagement. It's about maintaining the delicate balance between adhering to the project's initial scope and adapting to necessary changes. By effectively managing scope creep, a project manager can steer the project towards successful completion, ensuring it meets its objectives, stays within budget, and is delivered on time.

Project Scope Management Questions

1. What is the primary objective of Project Scope Management in project management?
2. How does detailed planning in Scope Management contribute to the success of a project?
3. What role does effective communication play in managing project scope?
4. Describe the concept of scope creep and its impact on project management.
5. What are the key steps in defining the project scope?
6. How is the Work Breakdown Structure (WBS) utilized in Scope Management?
7. What strategies can be employed to prevent scope creep in a project?
8. Why is stakeholder management important in controlling project scope?
9. Explain the significance of change control processes in Scope Management.
10. How does documentation aid in the process of Scope Management?

Project Scope Management Answers

1. Answer: The primary objective of Project Scope Management is to accurately define the boundaries of the project and control what is included in it. This involves identifying all the tasks, deliverables, and goals that form part of the project and distinguishing them from those that do not. Effective Scope Management ensures that the project focuses on its original objectives without straying into unrelated areas, which could lead to inefficiencies, cost overruns, or failure to meet core goals. It establishes a clear understanding among all stakeholders about what the project will deliver, contributing to focused efforts and efficient resource use.

2. Answer: Detailed planning in Scope Management is crucial for laying out a clear roadmap for project execution. This involves breaking down the overall project scope into smaller, more manageable components, often visualized through a Work Breakdown Structure (WBS). By defining these components, the project team can better allocate resources, assign tasks, and set realistic timelines. It helps in avoiding misunderstandings about project deliverables and ensures that all team members are aware of their responsibilities. This level of planning reduces risks of scope creep and ensures that each aspect of the project is aligned with its overall objectives, leading to a more organized and predictable project execution.

3. Answer: Effective communication is vital in managing project scope as it ensures that all stakeholders have a common understanding of what the project entails. Regular and clear communication about the project's progress and any changes in scope helps in managing expectations and prevents misunderstandings. It involves not only conveying information but also ensuring that it is received and understood by all parties involved. Effective communication facilitates transparency, allows for early detection and addressing of issues related to scope changes, and keeps everyone aligned with the project's objectives.

4. Answer: Scope creep refers to the incremental expansion of a project's scope without proper evaluation or adjustments to resources, time, and cost. It often occurs due to additional tasks or features being added to the project without proper authorization or consideration of their impact. Scope creep can lead to project delays, cost overruns, resource strain, and can even affect the quality of the final deliverable. If not managed effectively, it can significantly derail a project from its intended outcome, leading to

dissatisfaction among stakeholders and potentially causing the project to fail in achieving its original goals.

5. Answer: Defining the project scope involves several key steps: Firstly, engaging with stakeholders to understand their needs, expectations, and objectives for the project. Secondly, gathering and analyzing requirements to develop a clear understanding of what the project should achieve. Thirdly, documenting these requirements in a detailed scope statement which includes project boundaries, deliverables, constraints, and assumptions. Finally, getting approval from key stakeholders on this documented scope, ensuring that there is a mutual understanding and agreement on what the project will encompass.

6. Answer: The Work Breakdown Structure (WBS) is a key tool in Scope Management, used to decompose the project's scope into smaller, manageable components. It organizes and defines the total scope of the project, breaking it down into manageable tasks that can be scheduled, cost-estimated, monitored, and controlled. Each level of the WBS provides a more detailed segmentation of the project's scope, helping in assigning responsibilities, planning resources, and setting milestones. It serves as a framework for what needs to be delivered and helps in tracking project progress against the defined scope.

7. Answer: Preventing scope creep involves several strategies: Establishing a clear and detailed project scope from the outset and ensuring it is well communicated and understood by all stakeholders. Implementing robust change management processes where any changes to the scope are thoroughly evaluated for their impact on the project and approved through a formal process. Regular monitoring of project progress against the defined scope to detect any deviations early. Educating the project team and stakeholders about the implications of scope changes. And maintaining strong project leadership to make informed decisions on whether to accept or reject changes to the scope.

8. Answer: Stakeholder management is crucial in controlling project scope as stakeholders often have varying interests, expectations, and influences over the project. Effective management of these stakeholders helps in ensuring their needs and expectations are understood and managed appropriately. It involves regularly communicating with stakeholders about the project's progress, any changes in scope, and the reasons behind these changes. Managing stakeholders effectively can prevent unnecessary scope alterations driven by individual preferences and ensures that scope changes align with the overall project objectives.

9. Answer: Change control processes are essential in Scope Management to systematically manage any alterations to the project's scope. These processes ensure that every change is evaluated in terms of its impact on the project's schedule, cost, resources, and quality. It involves documenting the change, assessing its benefits and risks, obtaining necessary approvals, and updating the project plan to reflect the change. This formal approach prevents ad-hoc or uncontrolled changes, maintaining the integrity of the original project plan and objectives.

10. Answer: Documentation plays a pivotal role in Scope Management by providing a written record of the project's scope, agreements, and any changes that occur. Key documents include the project scope statement, WBS, and change request forms. These documents serve as a reference point throughout the project lifecycle, ensuring that all team members and stakeholders have a clear and common understanding of what the project entails. They also provide a basis for resolving discrepancies or misunderstandings about the scope and serve as evidence for decisions made during the project.

Chapter 6: Project Schedule Management

Advanced Concepts in Schedule Management

Schedule management is an art that requires a deep understanding of time as a resource. It's more than just plotting tasks on a timeline; it's about orchestrating various elements to ensure project completion in a timely and efficient manner. Advanced concepts in schedule management go beyond basic planning; they involve strategic foresight, flexibility, and a mastery of various tools and techniques.

At the core of advanced schedule management is the development of a comprehensive and realistic project timeline. This process is akin to composing a piece of music, where each note must be placed perfectly to create a harmonious melody. The project manager must understand the intricacies of the project's tasks, dependencies, and resources. This involves not just laying out the tasks but understanding their relationships and constraints. It's about visualizing the project as a whole and understanding how changes in one area can ripple through the entire project.

One of the critical aspects of advanced schedule management is the ability to balance flexibility with control. Projects often face unforeseen challenges and changes, and the schedule must be adaptable enough to accommodate these. However, this flexibility should not lead to a loss of control over the project timeline. Effective schedule management involves anticipating potential delays and building in buffer times, allowing for adjustments without derailing the overall project timeline.

Risk management plays a crucial role in schedule management. Advanced scheduling involves identifying potential risks to the project timeline and developing strategies to mitigate them. This proactive approach to risk management includes regular review of the project schedule to identify areas where risks could impact the timeline and taking preemptive action to address these risks. It's about staying one step ahead, ensuring that risks are managed before they become issues.

Another key aspect is the use of sophisticated scheduling tools and techniques. In the modern project management landscape, a variety of tools are available, ranging from simple Gantt charts to complex project management software. These tools provide capabilities for detailed scheduling, resource allocation, and progress tracking. The effective use of these tools requires not just technical proficiency but also an understanding of how to best apply them to the specific needs of the project.

Effective communication is integral to advanced schedule management. It involves keeping all stakeholders informed about the project schedule, any changes to it, and the reasons behind these changes. Clear communication ensures that everyone involved in the project understands the timeline, their roles, and responsibilities, and the impact of their work on the overall project schedule.

Advanced schedule management is a critical component of successful project execution. It requires a blend of strategic planning, flexibility, risk management, and effective use of scheduling tools. It's about seeing the big picture, understanding the intricacies of the project, and guiding it through to completion on time. By mastering advanced concepts in schedule management, a project manager can ensure that the project not only meets its deadlines but does so efficiently and effectively, maximizing resources and achieving its objectives.

Tools, Techniques, and Strategies for Schedule Development

Developing a project schedule is a task that combines the precision of a master craftsman with the foresight of a strategist. It's about crafting a timeline that not only maps out the journey of a project but also anticipates the possible twists and turns along the way. The creation of this schedule involves a blend of tools, techniques, and strategies, each playing a crucial role in transforming a project's objectives into a structured, executable plan.

The process begins with a thorough understanding of the project's scope. Like an architect who draws a building plan, the project manager first sketches out the project's objectives, deliverables, and major milestones. This initial step forms the backbone of the schedule, providing a framework upon which the finer details are added.

Next comes the layering of tasks. This stage involves breaking down the project's milestones into smaller, more manageable tasks. It's a meticulous process, akin to piecing together a complex puzzle. Each task is analyzed in terms of its duration, dependencies, and resources required. The project manager weaves these tasks together, creating a network that visually represents the project's workflow. This network not only shows the sequence of activities but also highlights the relationships between them, offering insight into how changes in one task might ripple through to others.

In this endeavor, the project manager employs various tools and techniques. Scheduling software has become a staple in modern project management, offering functionalities that range from simple Gantt charts to complex algorithms for resource allocation and risk assessment. These tools provide a digital canvas on which the project's timeline can be artfully drawn, edited, and refined. They offer the advantage of real-time updates and adjustments, allowing the schedule to evolve as the project progresses.

Yet, the use of these tools is not just about inputting data and tracking progress. It requires skill and judgment. The project manager must decide how to best utilize these tools to reflect the project's reality. They must balance the precision of the software with the fluidity of the project's dynamics. It involves making strategic decisions about task durations, allocating resources efficiently, and identifying critical paths – the sequence of tasks that determine the project's minimum duration.

One of the key strategies in schedule development is building in flexibility. Despite the best planning, projects often encounter unforeseen challenges that can impact the schedule. The project manager, therefore, plans for contingencies. This might involve buffer times for critical tasks or alternative pathways for task completion. It's about having a plan B (and sometimes a plan C), ensuring that the project remains on track even when faced with unexpected hurdles.

Effective communication is another critical strategy in schedule development. The project schedule should be a transparent and shared document, accessible to all team members and stakeholders. Regular updates, discussions, and feedback sessions ensure that everyone is aligned with the schedule and understands their role in it. It's about creating a collaborative environment where the schedule is not just a directive but a collective commitment.

The ongoing review and refinement of the schedule are crucial. The project manager regularly revisits the schedule, assessing its alignment with the project's progress and objectives. This iterative process is not just about tracking what has been done but also about anticipating future challenges and opportunities. It's a dynamic process, one that requires the project manager to be both reactive and proactive, adapting the schedule to the project's evolving needs.

Developing a project schedule is a complex yet essential task, requiring a careful blend of tools, techniques, and strategies. It involves detailed planning, strategic thinking, and continuous adaptation. By skillfully crafting and managing the project schedule, the project manager navigates the project through its many phases, ensuring that each step is taken at the right time and in the right way, leading to the successful completion of the project.

Expert Tips for Controlling and Managing Project Schedules

Controlling and managing project schedules is akin to steering a ship through constantly changing seas. It requires not only a firm hand at the helm but also the ability to foresee and adapt to the shifting tides and winds. Expert project managers understand that a project schedule is a living entity, one that needs continuous attention and fine-tuning to ensure the project reaches its destination successfully.

One of the cardinal rules in managing project schedules is to establish a solid foundation at the beginning. This involves creating a detailed and realistic schedule that accounts for all project activities, resources, and constraints. Much like an architect laying the groundwork for a building, this step is crucial in providing a stable base upon which the project can be built. The schedule should be comprehensive, yet flexible; detailed, yet not rigid. It's a delicate balance between precision and adaptability.

Once the schedule is set, the next step is vigilant monitoring. This ongoing process is more than just ticking off completed tasks; it's a critical examination of project progress against the planned schedule. Expert project managers use a variety of tools and techniques for this, from traditional Gantt charts to sophisticated project management software. These tools provide a visual representation of the project timeline, making it easier to spot delays or deviations. But tools alone are not enough; they need to be coupled with a keen understanding of the project's dynamics and the ability to read between the lines.

Effective communication is another key in managing project schedules. It involves keeping all stakeholders informed about the project's progress, challenges, and any deviations from the schedule. This transparency is crucial in managing expectations and fostering a collaborative environment. It also opens up avenues for feedback, providing insights that can help in adjusting the schedule as needed.

One of the more challenging aspects of schedule management is dealing with changes. Changes, whether they come from external factors or internal re-assessments, are inevitable in most projects. Expert project managers know that managing these changes is not just about accommodating them in the schedule; it's about evaluating their impact, understanding their implications, and making informed decisions. It's a process that requires a thorough understanding of the project's objectives and the ability to balance the new requirements with the existing ones.

Risk management is also an integral part of controlling and managing project schedules. Risks, both known and unknown, can have a significant impact on the project timeline. Expert project managers not only identify potential risks early on but also develop mitigation strategies to minimize their impact. This proactive approach to risk management is essential in keeping the project on track.

Another expert tip is to focus on the critical path of the project. Understanding which tasks are critical to the project's completion and which have some flexibility can be vital in making decisions when the schedule needs to be adjusted. It's about prioritizing tasks and resources in a way that ensures the project's key milestones are met.

Expert project managers know that the key to successful schedule management is flexibility and adaptability. Projects are dynamic, and what seemed like a well-laid plan at the beginning can quickly become obsolete as the project evolves. Being open to re-assessing and adjusting the schedule, while keeping the project's goals in focus, is crucial.

Controlling and managing project schedules is a complex task that requires a combination of detailed planning, continuous monitoring, effective communication, change management, and risk assessment. It demands not only technical skills and tools but also strategic thinking, adaptability, and a deep understanding of project dynamics. By mastering these aspects, expert project managers can guide their projects through the complexities and challenges of schedule management, ensuring timely and successful project completion.

Overcoming Common Scheduling Challenges

Navigating the often-turbulent waters of project scheduling is a task fraught with challenges, akin to a captain steering a ship through a storm. The art of scheduling is not just about plotting tasks on a timeline; it's about foreseeing obstacles, adapting to changes, and keeping the project on course. Common scheduling challenges, if not addressed astutely, can lead to delays, cost overruns, and even project failure.

One of the most significant challenges in project scheduling is the uncertainty that often clouds project timelines. Much like a weather forecast, a project schedule is based on assumptions and predictions which may not always hold true. Unexpected events, resource constraints, or technical difficulties can throw a carefully planned schedule off track. To navigate this uncertainty, project managers adopt a flexible approach. This involves building buffers into the schedule, allowing for some leeway in case of delays. It also means maintaining a constant vigil on the project's progress and being ready to make adjustments as needed.

Another frequent challenge is the misalignment of resources. Often, the resources available may not align perfectly with the project's demands. This could be due to the unavailability of key personnel, equipment, or other necessary inputs. Overcoming this challenge requires strategic resource management – carefully planning resource allocation, prioritizing tasks, and, if necessary, seeking additional resources or adjusting the project scope to match the available resources.

Scope creep is a notorious issue in project scheduling. It refers to the gradual expansion of the project's scope, often without corresponding adjustments in time, resources, and budget. Scope creep can stealthily derail a project, leading to a schedule that is constantly playing catch-up. Combating scope creep involves a combination of clear initial scope definition, effective change management processes, and strong stakeholder communication. It requires the project manager to be vigilant and decisive, ensuring that any changes to the project scope are carefully evaluated and managed.

Communication breakdowns also pose a significant challenge in scheduling. Miscommunication or lack of communication can lead to misunderstandings, missed deadlines, and tasks being executed incorrectly or out of sequence. Effective communication is key – ensuring that all team members, stakeholders, and vendors are on the same page regarding the project schedule. Regular meetings, clear documentation, and open lines of communication are essential tools in ensuring that information flows smoothly and accurately.

Finally, one of the more subtle challenges in project scheduling is the human factor. The motivations, work habits, and personal schedules of team members can greatly impact the project schedule. Overcoming this challenge involves understanding the team dynamics, setting realistic expectations, and providing support where needed. It's about creating a work environment where team members are motivated, their workload is manageable, and they have the necessary tools and support to complete their tasks on time.

Overcoming common scheduling challenges in project management requires a blend of strategic planning, flexibility, effective resource and communication management, and an understanding of team dynamics. It's about anticipating potential issues, adapting to changes, and maintaining a clear focus on the project goals. By skillfully navigating these challenges, project managers can keep their projects on track, ensuring successful and timely completion.

Project Schedule Management Questions

1. What is the primary goal of advanced project schedule management?
2. How does the development of a comprehensive project timeline contribute to schedule management?
3. Describe the balance between flexibility and control in effective schedule management.
4. What role does risk management play in project schedule management?
5. How are sophisticated scheduling tools and techniques utilized in advanced schedule management?
6. Why is effective communication integral to schedule management?
7. What is the importance of building flexibility into a project's schedule?
8. How can changes in project scheduling be effectively managed?
9. What strategies are essential for overcoming common scheduling challenges?
10. How does the human factor influence project scheduling?

Project Schedule Management Answers

1. Answer: The primary goal of advanced project schedule management is to orchestrate various project elements efficiently to ensure completion in a timely and effective manner, going beyond basic planning to strategic foresight and flexibility.

2. Answer: The development of a comprehensive project timeline allows for a clear visualization of the project as a whole, understanding task relationships and constraints, and seeing how changes in one area can affect the entire project, aiding in efficient orchestration of tasks.

3. Answer: In effective schedule management, balancing flexibility with control means adapting the schedule to unforeseen challenges while maintaining control over the timeline, including anticipating potential delays and building buffer times for adjustments.

4. Answer: In project schedule management, risk management involves identifying potential risks to the project timeline and developing strategies to mitigate them, ensuring that risks are managed proactively before they become issues.

5. Answer: Sophisticated scheduling tools and techniques provide capabilities for detailed scheduling, resource allocation, and progress tracking. They require technical proficiency and strategic application to the project's specific needs for effective utilization.

6. Answer: Effective communication in schedule management ensures all stakeholders are informed about the project schedule and any changes, maintaining transparency and alignment, and managing expectations.

7. Answer: Building flexibility into a project's schedule is important for allowing adjustments without derailing the overall timeline, accommodating unforeseen challenges while keeping the project on course.

8. Answer: Changes in project scheduling can be effectively managed through robust change management processes, evaluating the impact of changes, and making informed decisions on their incorporation, while updating the project plan and communicating these changes to stakeholders.

9. Answer: Essential strategies for overcoming common scheduling challenges include flexible and realistic initial scheduling, vigilant monitoring of progress, strategic resource management, effective communication, and proactive risk management.

10. Answer: The human factor influences project scheduling through team dynamics, individual work habits, motivations, and personal schedules, affecting task completion and overall project progress. It requires understanding team dynamics, setting realistic expectations, and providing necessary support

Chapter 7: Project Quality Management

Principles and Theories of Quality Management

The concept of quality management is like the spine of a grand narrative. It's not just a single chapter but a theme that runs throughout, crucial to the story's success. Quality management, rooted in principles and theories that have evolved over time, is fundamental in ensuring that a project not only meets but exceeds the expectations of its stakeholders.

The foundational principle of quality management is the understanding that quality is not an afterthought or a final check, but a continuous process. It's woven into every aspect of project management, from the initial planning stages to the final delivery. This principle asserts that quality should be built into the product or service from the outset, not inspected into it at the end. This proactive approach to quality is akin to a chef tasting the dish at every stage of preparation, ensuring that each ingredient contributes to the final flavor.

Central to quality management is the concept of customer satisfaction. The end goal of any project is not just to deliver a product or service but to fulfill, and ideally surpass, the expectations of the customer or end-user. This customer-centric approach drives the project's objectives, scope, and methodologies. It's about understanding the customer's needs and preferences and tailoring the project outputs to align with these requirements.

The theories of quality management have evolved through various schools of thought. One of the earliest and most influential was the work of W. Edwards Deming, who introduced the idea of quality being a continuous cycle (Plan-Do-Check-Act) and the importance of reducing variability in processes. Deming's theory underscored the idea that quality is not the responsibility of a specific department but a collective organizational commitment.

Following Deming, other theorists like Joseph Juran and Philip Crosby contributed to the quality management discourse. Juran emphasized the role of top management in quality control and the idea of quality planning, quality control, and quality improvement. Crosby introduced the concept of 'zero defects' and 'doing it right the first time,' highlighting the importance of striving for excellence and preventing mistakes before they occur.

Another significant theory in quality management is Total Quality Management (TQM). TQM is a holistic approach that focuses on long-term success through customer satisfaction and involves all members of an organization in improving processes, products, services, and culture. It's about creating a culture where quality is everyone's responsibility.

In the current landscape, quality management also incorporates Lean and Six Sigma methodologies. Lean focuses on eliminating waste and optimizing processes, while Six Sigma aims at reducing variation and improving process control. These methodologies offer tools and techniques to achieve high quality, efficiency, and customer satisfaction.

In conclusion, the principles and theories of quality management form an essential framework in project management. They emphasize that quality should be an integral part of every stage of a project, focused on meeting customer needs and expectations. From Deming's cycle to TQM, Lean, and Six Sigma, these theories provide a roadmap for embedding quality into the fabric of project management. They remind us that quality is not just a target to be achieved but a journey of continuous improvement.

Strategies for Planning and Implementing Quality in Projects

Quality, in the context of project management, is not a static feature but a dynamic attribute that evolves and adapts throughout the project's lifecycle. The strategies for planning and implementing quality in projects require a harmonious blend of foresight, precision, and adaptability.

At the very inception of a project, laying the groundwork for quality begins with a clear understanding of what quality means for that particular project. This initial step is like setting the parameters for a journey; it involves defining quality objectives based on the project's scope, stakeholder expectations, and industry standards. Quality in a construction project, for example, might revolve around safety and durability, while in a software development project, it might focus on user experience and performance. This understanding helps in creating a quality plan that serves as a blueprint for how these quality objectives will be achieved.

The development of a quality plan is a critical part of the planning process. This plan outlines the quality standards to be applied to the project and the methodologies to be used in achieving these standards. It involves identifying key quality metrics, setting up control processes, and defining acceptance criteria. But the plan is not a static document; it is a living guide that can adapt as the project progresses. It lays out how quality will be managed and assures all stakeholders that quality is a priority.

Effective implementation of quality in a project hinges on integrating quality management practices into every phase of the project. From the initial design and planning stages to execution and closure, quality should be a thread that runs through all activities. This integration means that quality is not an additional layer added at the end, but a core component of all project processes. It's about building quality into the project, not inspecting it in at the end.

One of the key strategies in implementing quality is the practice of continuous monitoring and control. This process involves regularly evaluating the project's outputs against the established quality standards. Monitoring tools and techniques like audits, reviews, and inspections are used to assess quality continuously. This ongoing evaluation helps in identifying any deviations from the set quality standards and allows for immediate corrective actions.

Engaging the project team in quality management is another vital strategy. Quality is not the sole responsibility of a quality manager or department; it's a collective responsibility of everyone involved in the project. Training and involving the team in quality processes ensure that they understand the quality objectives, the importance of meeting these standards, and their role in maintaining quality throughout the project.

Stakeholder involvement is also crucial in planning and implementing quality. Regular communication with stakeholders about quality expectations, progress, and any issues ensures that there are no surprises at the end of the project. It also allows for the incorporation of stakeholder feedback, which can be crucial in aligning the project's outputs with their expectations.

Lastly, a critical strategy in quality implementation is the use of feedback loops for continuous improvement. Lessons learned from quality assessments and stakeholder feedback should be fed back into the project processes. This approach ensures that the project not only maintains its current level of quality but also improves over time.

Planning and implementing quality in projects is a complex but essential aspect of project management. It requires a strategic approach that integrates quality into every phase of the project, continuous monitoring and control, team and stakeholder involvement, and a commitment to continuous improvement. By embedding these strategies into the project management process, the project team can ensure that the final deliverables meet the desired quality standards, thereby achieving customer satisfaction and project success.

Quality Control and Assurance: Advanced Techniques

Advanced techniques in quality control and assurance are crucial in ensuring that a project not only meets but exceeds its quality benchmarks, delivering exceptional value to stakeholders and customers.

This process is more than just a series of checks and balances; it's a comprehensive approach to ensure that every product or service delivered by the project aligns with the defined quality standards. Advanced quality control techniques involve a combination of rigorous testing, detailed inspections, and statistical methods. Like an artist scrutinizing every stroke on a canvas, quality control specialists examine every aspect of the project deliverables to ensure they meet the desired specifications.

One advanced technique in quality control is the use of statistical quality control (SQC). This method employs statistical methods to monitor and control the quality of the project's outputs. SQC involves analyzing data collected from various stages of the project to identify trends, variances, and potential areas of improvement. It's an approach that allows project managers to make data-driven decisions, enhancing the project's overall quality.

Quality assurance, on the other hand, takes a broader view. It focuses on the processes used in the project to ensure quality is maintained throughout the project's lifecycle. Quality assurance is about instilling a culture of quality in the team, ensuring that every process, from initial planning to final delivery, is conducted in a manner that upholds the project's quality standards. Advanced techniques in quality assurance involve process audits, reviews, and the implementation of quality management systems.

One such advanced technique is Total Quality Management (TQM). TQM is a holistic approach that focuses on long-term success through customer satisfaction and involves all members of an organization in improving processes, products, services, and culture. It's about creating a culture where quality is everyone's responsibility. TQM integrates quality principles into all aspects of the project, from design to delivery, ensuring that quality is a continuous pursuit.

Another advanced approach in quality assurance is the implementation of Six Sigma methodologies. Six Sigma is a disciplined, data-driven approach for eliminating defects in any process. It provides project managers with a set of tools and techniques to improve the capability of their business processes, aiming for near-perfection in quality delivery. This approach is about precision and striving for the highest standards of quality.

Both quality control and assurance are enhanced by the integration of technology. Advanced software tools offer sophisticated ways to track quality, analyze data, and report findings. These tools provide a comprehensive platform for managing all aspects of quality in a project, from tracking defects to conducting root cause analysis.

Advanced techniques in quality control and assurance are essential in elevating the quality of project deliverables. They involve a combination of meticulous evaluation, process improvement, cultural change, and the use of sophisticated tools and methodologies. By implementing these techniques, project managers can ensure that their projects not only meet the required standards but also deliver exceptional quality, leading to customer satisfaction and project success. Quality control and assurance, thus, are not just functions within a project; they are foundational elements that define its overall success and impact.

Case Studies: Quality Management Success and Failures

Exploring a few such case studies offers insights into the pivotal role of quality management in determining a project's success or failure.

1. In the automotive industry, there's an exemplary case of success rooted in quality management. A prominent car manufacturer, once plagued by significant quality issues, experienced a downturn in customer satisfaction and brand reputation. The pivotal change occurred with the embrace of Total Quality Management (TQM) practices. This shift initiated an extensive revamp of their quality management processes, deeply engaging every tier of the workforce, from assembly line employees to top executives, in a culture dedicated to perpetual enhancement.

   The manufacturer instituted stringent quality control measures and an extensive employee training and involvement program. These efforts led to a significant turnaround, not just in terms of vehicle quality but also in rebuilding customer confidence and establishing a robust competitive advantage in the marketplace. This transformation serves as a testament to the impact of thoroughly integrating quality management into all facets of a company's operations. It underscores that a holistic commitment to quality can catalyze substantial improvements, transcending the basic fulfillment of standards to achieve remarkable levels of excellence and customer trust.

2. In the software industry, there's a notable instance of project failure that underscores the consequences of poor quality management. A leading technology company, known for its software prowess, faced a significant setback with the release of a major software update. This update, despite undergoing extensive testing, was marred with bugs and performance issues, severely impacting the user experience.

   The critical flaws that eluded the testing phase led to widespread user dissatisfaction and substantial financial losses for the company. Upon analysis, the root cause of this failure was identified as inadequate quality assurance procedures, compounded by the pressure to adhere to aggressive release deadlines. This haste resulted in a compromised testing phase, where critical issues were overlooked.

   This incident serves as a stark reminder of the risks associated with prioritizing schedule adherence or cost-cutting over quality. It highlights the indispensable nature of thorough and effective quality assurance practices in software development. Furthermore, it illustrates the necessity of finding a balance between speed and quality, emphasizing that the pursuit of rapid deployment should not overshadow the fundamental need for delivering a reliable and high-quality product. This case exemplifies the pivotal role of robust quality management in safeguarding against such failures and ensuring the success and reliability of software products in a competitive market.

3. In the construction sector, a salient case study highlights the critical importance of quality management in large-scale projects. A high-profile infrastructure project, notable for its ambitious scope and stringent timeline, encountered severe quality challenges. These challenges stemmed from the complex nature of the project, which involved numerous subcontractors, each with their unique processes and standards.

   The primary issue was traced back to inadequate communication and coordination among these various parties. Additionally, the lack of a centralized quality control system further exacerbated the situation.

This absence of cohesive management and unified standards led to inconsistencies in quality across different aspects of the project.

As a result, the project faced not only significant delays but also substantial cost overruns. Beyond the immediate financial impact, there was considerable reputational damage, which is often harder to quantify and rectify. This case underlines the imperative need for clear, effective communication channels and a unified approach to quality control in large-scale construction projects.

It demonstrates that when dealing with complex projects involving multiple stakeholders, a centralized system of quality management is essential. Such a system ensures consistency and adherence to standards across all segments of the project. This case acts as a crucial lesson for the construction industry, emphasizing that while ambitious scales and tight timelines are challenging, they should not compromise the integral aspects of quality management and effective communication.

These case studies paint a vivid picture of the critical nature of quality management in projects. The lessons they impart are clear: embedding quality into the very fabric of project processes leads to success, while overlooking quality can result in failure. They also highlight the need for a holistic approach to quality management – one that encompasses not just processes and tools but also people and culture. In sum, quality management is not just a set of practices; it's a philosophy that, when embraced and implemented effectively, can lead to outstanding project outcomes and long-term success.

Project Quality Management Questions

1. What is the foundational principle of quality management in project management?
2. How does customer satisfaction relate to quality management in projects?
3. Who introduced the concept of the quality being a continuous cycle and what does it entail?
4. Explain Joseph Juran's and Philip Crosby's contributions to quality management theories.
5. What is Total Quality Management (TQM), and how does it approach quality?
6. How do Lean and Six Sigma methodologies fit into quality management?
7. What are the key steps in planning quality in a project?
8. How is continuous monitoring crucial in quality control?
9. What role does team involvement play in quality assurance?
10. Why are feedback loops important in maintaining and improving quality in projects?

Project Quality Management Answers

1. Answer: The foundational principle of quality management is that quality is not an afterthought or a final check but a continuous process integrated into every aspect of project management, from initial planning to final delivery.

2. Answer: In quality management, customer satisfaction is the end goal, driving the project's objectives, scope, and methodologies to ensure the project not only delivers what is promised but exceeds stakeholder expectations.

3. Answer: W. Edwards Deming introduced the idea of quality as a continuous cycle, known as Plan-Do-Check-Act. This cycle emphasizes constant improvement and reducing variability in processes, making quality a collective organizational commitment.

4. Answer: Joseph Juran emphasized the role of top management in quality control and the importance of quality planning, quality control, and quality improvement. Philip Crosby introduced the concepts of 'zero defects' and 'doing it right the first time,' focusing on preventing mistakes and striving for excellence.

5. Answer: Total Quality Management (TQM) is a holistic approach that focuses on long-term success through customer satisfaction, involving all members of an organization in improving processes, products, services, and culture, making quality everyone's responsibility.

6. Answer: Lean methodology focuses on eliminating waste and optimizing processes, while Six Sigma aims at reducing variation and improving process control. Both methodologies offer tools and techniques to achieve high quality and efficiency in projects.

7. Answer: Planning quality in a project involves defining quality objectives based on the project's scope, stakeholder expectations, and industry standards, and creating a quality plan that outlines the quality standards, control processes, and acceptance criteria.

8. Answer: Continuous monitoring in quality control involves regularly evaluating the project's outputs against established quality standards using tools like audits and inspections, allowing for immediate corrective actions to maintain quality.

9. Answer: Team involvement in quality assurance ensures that quality objectives and processes are understood and embraced by everyone involved in the project, promoting a culture where quality is a collective priority and responsibility.

10. Answer: Feedback loops are important in quality management as they allow for continuous improvement. Lessons learned and stakeholder feedback are used to refine and enhance project processes, ensuring ongoing enhancement of quality standards.

Chapter 8: Project Cost Management

Detailed Analysis of Cost Management in Projects

Cost management plays a pivotal role, akin to a meticulous choreographer ensuring every move is on budget and aligned with the project's financial constraints. This aspect of project management, when executed with precision and insight, can be the difference between a project's success and its downfall.

It involves a comprehensive understanding of all the financial aspects of a project, from initial estimates to final accounting. Imagine constructing a building; just as an architect considers the cost of materials, labor, and contingencies, a project manager must account for all the resources, personnel, and potential risks that could impact the project's cost.

The journey of effective cost management begins with the meticulous process of cost estimation. This initial step is crucial as it sets the financial framework for the project. Estimation is more art than science, requiring the project manager to balance historical data with future predictions, considering variables such as resource availability, market trends, and technological advancements. It's a delicate balancing act, where underestimation can lead to budget overruns and overestimation can render the project unfeasible.

Following the estimation, the next stage is the allocation of the budget. This step involves distributing the estimated cost across the various elements of the project. It's like painting a canvas, where the project manager uses the budget to bring the picture of the project to life, ensuring that each aspect receives adequate financial attention. This allocation must be realistic and flexible, allowing for adjustments as the project evolves.

Once the project is underway, cost control becomes the focal point. This ongoing process is akin to navigating a ship through stormy seas, where vigilance and adaptability are key. The project manager must continuously monitor expenditures, ensuring that the project stays within its financial boundaries. This monitoring is not just about tracking costs but also about foreseeing potential overruns and taking preemptive measures to mitigate them. It involves a thorough understanding of the project's progress, comparing actual expenses with the budget, and making adjustments as necessary.

Effective cost management also entails dealing with changes and unforeseen expenses. Changes are inevitable in any project, and the project manager must have a robust process for managing these changes without derailing the budget. This involves evaluating the financial impact of changes, seeking additional funding if necessary, and re-allocating the budget to accommodate these changes.

Expert Techniques in Estimating and Budgeting Project Costs

The art of estimating and budgeting project costs stands as a testament to a manager's foresight and precision. This task is much like an artist delicately balancing colors on a palette, aiming to create a masterpiece without extravagance. Expert techniques in estimating and budgeting project costs require a blend of analytical acumen, market insight, and strategic foresight.

At the outset, estimating project costs is an intricate dance with uncertainty. It involves predicting future expenditures in a landscape often riddled with unforeseen challenges. Expert project managers approach this with a combination of tools and methodologies, each offering a lens through which the financial landscape of a project can be discerned. They delve into historical data, drawing insights from past projects to inform the present. This historical analysis is not just about replicating past budgets but understanding the nuances and learning from previous experiences.

Another pivotal aspect of expert cost estimation is the detailed analysis of project requirements. This process involves breaking down the project into its constituent tasks and components. Like a chef deconstructing a recipe into ingredients and steps, a project manager dissects the project to understand every requirement's cost implications. This breakdown is meticulously detailed, encompassing materials, labor, equipment, and other resources needed for the project.

Market analysis also plays a crucial role in cost estimation. Costs are not static; they are subject to market fluctuations and economic trends. Expert project managers keep a keen eye on market conditions, understanding how factors like supply chain disruptions, inflation rates, or labor market trends can impact project costs. This vigilance ensures that estimations are not only based on historical data but are also attuned to current market realities.

Risk analysis is another critical component of expert cost estimation. Every project carries its own set of risks, and these potential pitfalls can significantly impact costs. Expert project managers employ risk analysis techniques to identify and assess potential risks, from resource availability issues to regulatory changes. They then factor these risks into the cost estimation, often setting aside contingencies to cushion the project from these financial uncertainties.

Once the cost estimation is completed, the next phase is budgeting. Budgeting is more than just allocating funds; it's about strategically distributing resources to achieve the project's objectives. This stage requires a deep understanding of the project's priorities and constraints. Expert project managers use their cost estimations to create a budget that aligns with the project's goals, ensuring that every dollar spent contributes to the project's success.

Throughout the process, expert project managers maintain a balance between precision and flexibility. They understand that while detailed estimations and budgets are crucial, rigidity can be detrimental. Projects are dynamic, and conditions can change. Therefore, they regularly revisit and adjust the cost estimations and budgets, maintaining a delicate balance between adhering to financial constraints and adapting to evolving project needs.

Expert techniques in estimating and budgeting project costs are integral to the success of any project. They involve a comprehensive approach that combines historical analysis, detailed requirement breakdown, market analysis, risk assessment, and strategic budgeting. By adeptly navigating these aspects, expert project managers ensure that their projects are not only financially viable but also optimized for efficiency and effectiveness. This meticulous approach to cost estimation and budgeting is what transforms a project from a mere plan into a feasible, financially sound venture.

Innovative Cost Control Techniques

The mastery of cost control stands as a crucial determinant of a project's success. This aspect of project management, akin to navigating a ship through turbulent waters, demands not only precision but also innovation. As projects become increasingly complex and budgets tighter, project managers are turning to innovative cost control techniques to ensure financial efficiency and effectiveness.

The essence of innovative cost control lies in a proactive rather than reactive approach. This mindset shift is like a chess player anticipating moves ahead, rather than just reacting to the opponent's moves. It involves forecasting potential financial issues and implementing strategies to mitigate them before they escalate into significant problems. Advanced forecasting tools, leveraging data analytics and predictive modeling, enable project managers to foresee cost overruns and take preemptive action. These tools analyze historical data, current project metrics, and market trends, providing a detailed prognosis of the project's financial health.

Another key aspect of innovative cost control is the integration of real-time financial tracking. In a traditional setup, cost tracking often lags behind the actual spending, leading to delayed responses to budget overruns. By utilizing real-time tracking technologies, project managers can monitor expenditures as they occur. This immediate insight allows for swift adjustments and decision-making, ensuring that the project remains within its financial boundaries. Real-time tracking tools can be integrated with project management software, providing a comprehensive view of both project progress and financial status.

Adopting a Lean approach to project management is also an innovative technique in cost control. Lean project management focuses on maximizing value while minimizing waste. This approach is not just about cutting costs but about optimizing processes, resources, and time. Lean techniques such as value stream mapping, 5S (Sort, Set in order, Shine, Standardize, Sustain), and Kaizen (continuous improvement) can be applied to identify inefficiencies and streamline processes, leading to cost savings without compromising the project's quality or objectives.

Collaborative cost management is another innovative technique gaining traction. This approach involves engaging all project stakeholders, including team members, suppliers, and clients, in the cost management process. Collaborative cost management is like conducting an orchestra where each musician's input contributes to the symphony's overall success. By involving stakeholders in cost discussions, project managers can tap into a wealth of ideas and insights for cost-saving opportunities. This collaboration can lead to innovative solutions such as co-designing with suppliers to reduce costs or redefining scope with clients to align with budget constraints.

Agile methodologies, traditionally associated with project management flexibility and efficiency, also offer innovative avenues for cost control. Agile's iterative approach, with its regular reviews and adaptations, allows for constant cost reassessment and realignment. By breaking the project into smaller, manageable segments (sprints), project managers can monitor and control costs more closely, adjusting the budget and scope as the project evolves.

Lastly, risk management plays a pivotal role in innovative cost control. Advanced risk management techniques involve not just identifying potential risks but also quantifying their financial impact and developing strategies to mitigate them. This process includes scenario planning, sensitivity analysis, and contingency planning. By proactively managing risks, project managers can prevent cost overruns and ensure financial stability.

Innovative cost control techniques are essential in the modern landscape of project management. They combine advanced technologies, Lean principles, collaborative approaches, Agile methodologies, and proactive risk management to maintain financial discipline. These techniques are not just about keeping the project within budget; they're about enhancing value, optimizing resources, and ensuring the project's financial success. As projects continue to grow in complexity and scale, these innovative approaches will become increasingly critical in steering projects to successful and financially sound completions.

Real-world Examples of Cost Management Challenges

The world of project management is replete with stories that illustrate the complexity and challenges of cost management. These real-world examples not only provide a glimpse into the hurdles that projects often encounter but also serve as cautionary tales that underscore the importance of effective cost management.

1. The case of a major bridge construction project serves as a quintessential example of cost management challenges in large infrastructure endeavors. Initially estimated at several million dollars with a three-year completion timeline, the project encountered various unforeseen complications. Key among these were geological challenges that were not anticipated in the initial planning phase. These issues necessitated additional engineering solutions, leading to a spike in labor costs as well as extended time requirements.

    Simultaneously, the project was impacted by evolving environmental regulations. These changes in the regulatory landscape demanded compliance measures that were not accounted for in the original budget or timeline. Consequently, the project's expenses escalated significantly beyond the initial estimates, and the timeline for completion was stretched far beyond its initial projection.

    This scenario had a ripple effect, extending beyond financial implications to include public and stakeholder scrutiny. The stakeholders, ranging from investors to future users of the bridge, grew increasingly concerned about the escalating costs and the project's delayed timeline.

    This case underscores the critical nature of dynamic and flexible cost management strategies in large-scale projects. It highlights the importance of incorporating contingency plans for unforeseen challenges, both in terms of financial resources and project scheduling. Additionally, it emphasizes the need for continuous monitoring and adaptation of cost management plans in response to evolving project conditions, regulatory environments, and market factors. Effective cost management in such scenarios requires not only meticulous initial planning but also the agility to adapt to unforeseen changes and challenges that inevitably arise in complex, large-scale projects.

2. In the technology sector, a notable case study involves a tech company's venture into developing a new software platform, with ambitions to make a groundbreaking impact in the market. The project was launched with initial cost estimates anchored to aggressive, perhaps overly optimistic timelines. These estimations, however, fell short in accurately accounting for the complexities involved in integrating diverse technologies.

    As the development unfolded, the team encountered a series of technical challenges that were not fully anticipated. These difficulties, combined with an expanding scope – a phenomenon often referred to as 'scope creep' – resulted in significant delays. The ripple effect of these delays was twofold: not only did the project timeline extend, but there was also a substantial surge in costs.

    Confronted with these unanticipated challenges, the company found itself in a position where it was imperative to infuse additional funds. This decision to allocate more resources, while necessary to keep the project afloat and moving towards completion, had a marked impact on the company's overall financial health.

    This case exemplifies the inherent complexities and uncertainties involved in managing costs for projects that are driven by innovation, particularly in the technology sector. It illustrates how rapidly evolving project scopes and technical demands can escalate costs unexpectedly. This scenario reinforces the importance of adaptable and forward-looking cost management strategies, especially in sectors where technological advancement and innovation are at the forefront. It highlights the necessity for project managers to have a robust mechanism for monitoring and controlling costs, allowing for flexibility and responsiveness to change, and emphasizes the need for thorough risk assessment and contingency planning to accommodate the dynamic nature of technology projects.

3. The expansion endeavor of a global retailer in the retail sector offers a compelling study in the complexities of cost management in projects with an international scope. This ambitious project involved opening new stores across various global locations, each presenting its own set of challenges.

One of the primary hurdles encountered was the logistical complexities inherent in international projects. These ranged from coordinating construction efforts across different time zones to managing a diverse workforce. Additionally, the retailer faced regulatory challenges unique to each location, which were not fully anticipated in the initial planning stages.

A significant factor impacting the project's cost management was the variance in construction costs across different regions. These discrepancies arose from differences in local labor costs, material prices, and construction standards. Furthermore, the project was affected by fluctuations in currency exchange rates, which introduced financial unpredictability and complicated budgeting efforts.

Unexpected legal and compliance costs also emerged as a critical issue. These costs were associated with navigating the distinct legal frameworks and compliance requirements in each international location, adding an additional layer of complexity to the financial management of the project.

Faced with these multifaceted challenges, the retailer was compelled to reevaluate its expansion strategy. This reevaluation involved making strategic decisions on which store locations to prioritize and which to defer, based on a careful analysis of potential return on investment, market dynamics, and financial feasibility.

This case exemplifies the intricate nature of managing costs in global projects, where geopolitical dynamics, market variability, and regional differences significantly influence financial planning and decision-making. It highlights the necessity for comprehensive and adaptable cost management strategies that can accommodate the diverse and often unpredictable variables present in international project settings. Such strategies are crucial for navigating the myriad financial challenges and ensuring the successful execution and completion of projects with a global footprint.

4. The renovation project of a hospital in the healthcare industry offers a vivid illustration of the unique cost management challenges encountered in this sector. The project's primary objective was to modernize facilities and integrate cutting-edge technology to enhance patient care and operational efficiency. However, as the project progressed, several unforeseen challenges emerged, significantly impacting the cost management plan.

A critical oversight in the initial stages was underestimating the costs associated with procuring specialized equipment. Healthcare technology often involves advanced, high-cost apparatuses tailored to specific medical needs. This miscalculation was compounded by the stringent quality and compliance standards required for healthcare facilities, which necessitated additional investments to ensure that the renovated spaces met these rigorous criteria.

Moreover, the project faced unexpected disruptions in the supply chain. These disruptions, triggered by external events beyond the control of the project managers, resulted in escalated material costs. The increase in material costs was not accounted for in the initial budget, leading to a substantial financial strain.

As a consequence of these challenges, the project's budget had to be revised significantly upwards. This revision necessitated the hospital to seek additional funding sources, which posed its own set of complexities. Besides the financial implications, the project also caused operational disruptions. These disruptions affected the hospital's ability to provide services during the renovation period, adding another layer of complexity to the project management.

This hospital renovation project underscores the intricate challenges of cost management in healthcare projects. It highlights the importance of comprehensive planning that accounts for the specialized needs and high standards of healthcare facilities. Furthermore, it emphasizes the need for adaptable budgeting strategies that can accommodate unforeseen costs and disruptions, particularly in sectors where quality and compliance are paramount. This case study serves as a reminder of the critical nature of precise and flexible cost management in ensuring the successful completion of projects in the healthcare industry, where the stakes include not only financial outcomes but also the quality of patient care and services.

These real-world examples from diverse industries illustrate the multifaceted nature of cost management challenges in projects. They highlight the need for rigorous planning, comprehensive risk assessment, and adaptable cost management strategies. These stories also emphasize the importance of continually monitoring and revising cost estimates throughout the project's lifecycle to ensure alignment with the project's goals and external realities. Effective cost management is not just about sticking to a budget; it's about navigating the complexities of the project environment and making informed decisions to ensure financial sustainability and project success.

Project Cost Management Questions

1. What is the primary objective of cost management in project management?
2. How does cost estimation at the beginning of a project set the stage for effective cost management?
3. What is the importance of budget allocation in project cost management?
4. Describe the role of cost control in the lifecycle of a project.
5. How do changes and unforeseen expenses impact project cost management?
6. What are the key elements involved in the process of cost estimation?
7. How does market analysis influence cost estimation in project management?
8. Explain the significance of risk analysis in the cost estimation process.
9. What role does real-time financial tracking play in project cost management?
10. How can project managers effectively handle changes in project costs?

Project Cost Management Answers

1. Answer: The primary objective of cost management in project management is to ensure that the project is completed within the prescribed budget. This involves planning, estimating, budgeting, and controlling costs so that the project can be completed without unnecessary overruns.

2. Answer: Cost estimation at the beginning of a project sets the financial framework for the project. It involves predicting the monetary resources needed, which helps in creating a realistic budget and setting financial boundaries for the project.

3. Answer: Budget allocation in project cost management is crucial as it involves distributing the estimated cost across various elements of the project. This step ensures that each aspect of the project receives the necessary financial resources and helps in preventing over-expenditure in any single area.

4. Answer: Cost control in a project's lifecycle involves continuously monitoring expenditures and ensuring that the project stays within its financial boundaries. This process includes identifying and addressing any deviations from the budget and making adjustments to avoid budget overruns.

5. Answer: Changes and unforeseen expenses can significantly impact project cost management by causing deviations from the planned budget. Project managers must have robust processes to manage these changes, ensuring they evaluate the financial impact and make necessary budget adjustments.

6. Answer: The key elements in cost estimation include analyzing project requirements, understanding resource needs, and considering potential risks. This process requires a deep understanding of the project's scope and an analysis of historical data, market conditions, and resource availability.

7. Answer: Market analysis influences cost estimation by providing insights into current market conditions that can affect project costs, such as material costs, labor rates, and economic trends. This analysis helps ensure that cost estimations are realistic and reflective of current market realities.

8. Answer: Risk analysis in cost estimation involves identifying potential risks that could impact the project costs and assessing their likelihood and potential impact. This analysis helps in setting contingencies and making informed budgeting decisions to cushion the project from financial uncertainties.

9. Answer: Real-time financial tracking allows project managers to monitor expenditures as they occur, providing immediate insight into the project's financial status. This enables quick adjustments and decision-making, helping to keep the project within its budget.

10. Answer: Project managers can effectively handle changes in project costs by employing a structured change management process. This involves evaluating the impact of each change, deciding whether to incorporate it, and updating the budget accordingly. Effective communication with stakeholders about these changes is also crucial.

Chapter 9: Project Communication Management

The Role of Effective Communication in Projects

Effective communication is the golden thread that binds various elements of a project together. It's a pivotal component that, when executed skillfully, can significantly enhance the chances of a project's success. Just as a conductor communicates with an orchestra to create a harmonious symphony, a project manager uses effective communication to synchronize team efforts, align stakeholder expectations, and guide a project to successful completion.

At the heart of effective communication in projects is the ability to convey ideas, expectations, and information in a clear and understandable manner. This aspect of communication is crucial in setting the foundation for the project. It involves articulating the project goals, scope, and objectives in a way that is accessible to all team members and stakeholders, irrespective of their background or expertise. This initial communication sets the tone for the entire project, ensuring that everyone starts on the same page and understands what the project aims to achieve.

As the project progresses, communication becomes the vehicle for navigating the complexities and challenges that arise. It is the medium through which project managers coordinate tasks, convey changes, and resolve conflicts. Regular updates and discussions help in maintaining transparency, building trust, and fostering a collaborative environment. This continuous flow of information ensures that all involved parties are aware of the project's progress and any issues that need attention.

Effective communication in projects also involves actively listening to team members, stakeholders, and clients. This two-way communication process allows project managers to gather valuable feedback, understand concerns, and address them promptly. It's a dynamic interaction, where listening is as important as conveying information. By being receptive to feedback and suggestions, project managers can make informed decisions that reflect the collective input of the entire project team.

Moreover, communication in project management extends beyond verbal and written exchanges. It encompasses non-verbal cues, tone of voice, and even the medium chosen to convey the message. The choice between an email, a phone call, or a face-to-face meeting can significantly impact how the message is received and interpreted. Skilled project managers understand the nuances of these different communication methods and choose the most effective one based on the message's content and the audience.

In crisis situations or when dealing with difficult news, the importance of effective communication becomes even more pronounced. It's about delivering clear, concise, and honest information, even when the message is not positive. This transparency helps in building trust and credibility, which are crucial for navigating through challenging phases of the project.

The role of effective communication in project management cannot be overstated. It's an art that encompasses clarity, consistency, and responsiveness. Effective communication acts as a bridge connecting various stakeholders, a tool for resolving conflicts, a means for conveying vision and updates, and a method for building and maintaining a cohesive and motivated team. In essence, communication is not just a part of project management; it's the lifeline that ensures the health and success of a project from inception to completion.

Planning and Executing Project Communication Strategies

Communication strategies are the conductor's baton, guiding the melody of interactions and information flow. Effective planning and execution of these strategies are essential for maintaining harmony among team members and stakeholders. This process is not just about talking and listening but orchestrating a comprehensive approach that ensures every note of communication contributes to the project's success.

The planning of project communication strategies begins with an understanding of the project's landscape - its objectives, stakeholders, and potential challenges. Just as a cartographer charts a map, the project manager must outline a communication plan that considers who needs to receive information, the type of information to be shared, the frequency of communication, and the channels to be used. This plan is tailored to the project's unique environment, ensuring that the right messages reach the right people at the right time.

Central to this planning is stakeholder analysis. Every stakeholder has different needs and preferences for communication. Some may prefer detailed reports, while others might need only high-level summaries. Understanding these preferences is key to designing an effective communication strategy. It's like tuning an instrument to the right pitch - each stakeholder's frequency of information needs to be just right.

Another crucial aspect is determining the communication channels and tools. In today's digital world, options abound from emails and instant messaging to video conferences and collaborative online platforms. The choice of tools depends on the nature of the information, the urgency, and the audience's preferences. For instance, complex issues may require face-to-face meetings or video calls, while regular updates might be efficiently handled via emails or project management software.

Once the plan is in place, executing the communication strategy becomes the focus. This execution is more than disseminating information; it's about ensuring clarity, understanding, and engagement. Regular team meetings, stakeholder updates, and progress reports are common elements of this execution. These interactions are opportunities not just to share information but to foster a culture of openness, where feedback is encouraged, and concerns can be raised.

Effective execution also involves adaptability. Projects are dynamic, and communication needs can change. The project manager must be vigilant, ready to adjust the communication strategy as the project evolves. This flexibility is key in dealing with unexpected challenges or changes in the project scope.

Monitoring and evaluating the effectiveness of the communication strategy is another important element. This involves seeking feedback from team members and stakeholders, assessing the effectiveness of communication channels, and making adjustments as necessary. It's a continuous process, much like fine-tuning an instrument, ensuring that the communication strategy remains effective throughout the project lifecycle.

In crisis situations or when dealing with sensitive information, the communication strategy takes on even greater significance. In these instances, the project manager must ensure that communication is clear, timely, and, above all, transparent. It's about maintaining trust and credibility, even under challenging circumstances.

Planning and executing project communication strategies is a critical component of successful project management. It requires a thoughtful approach that considers the needs and preferences of stakeholders, the appropriate use of communication channels, and the flexibility to adapt to changing project dynamics. By effectively planning and executing these strategies, a project manager can ensure a steady flow of information, foster collaboration and trust, and steer the project towards its objectives, much like a conductor leading an orchestra to a harmonious and triumphant finale.

Communication Methods and Tools: Best Practices

Communication is the lifeline that ensures the smooth flow of information and maintains the cohesiveness of teams and stakeholders. The methods and tools of communication in projects are as varied as the colors on an artist's palette, each serving a unique purpose and contributing to the creation of a successful project narrative. Embracing best practices in these communication methods and tools is crucial for efficient and effective information exchange.

The approach oscillates between traditional face-to-face interactions and modern digital platforms. Face-to-face meetings, whether formal or informal, remain a vital method for complex discussions, conflict resolution, and building relationships. The power of personal interaction in conveying nuances, understanding body language, and fostering trust is unmatched. Best practices in these meetings include setting clear agendas, ensuring participant preparedness, and summarizing key decisions and action items.

Conversely, the digital revolution has introduced a plethora of tools that have transformed project communication. Email, for instance, remains a staple for formal and documented communication. Its effectiveness lies in its ability to convey clear and concise information, provide records of exchanges, and reach multiple individuals simultaneously. Best practices for email communication include keeping messages brief and to the point, using clear subject lines, and being mindful of the tone, as emails lack the nuance of verbal communication.

In recent years, instant messaging platforms and collaboration tools have become integral to project communication. These tools, such as Slack, Microsoft Teams, or Asana, offer instant, real-time communication and are ideal for quick updates, clarifications, or team collaboration. They break down the barriers of geography and time zones, allowing for seamless collaboration among global teams. Best practices here include establishing norms for their use, ensuring messages are professional and relevant, and integrating these tools with project management software for a unified communication approach.

Video conferencing tools have also become increasingly important, especially in the context of remote work and global teams. Platforms like Zoom, Skype, or Webex facilitate face-to-face interactions virtually, offering a more personal touch than emails or texts. They are particularly effective for team meetings, stakeholder updates, or brainstorming sessions. The best practices for video conferencing include testing technology beforehand, ensuring a quiet environment, and being attentive and engaged during calls.

Beyond these methods and tools, the best practices in project communication also emphasize the importance of active listening. Active listening involves fully concentrating, understanding, responding, and then remembering what is being said. It is fundamental in ensuring effective two-way communication, building trust, and ensuring that all team members and stakeholders feel heard and valued.

Another critical aspect is communication adaptability. Project managers must be adept at choosing the right communication tool and style depending on the situation, the message's urgency, and the audience's preferences. For instance, critical issues may warrant a face-to-face meeting, whereas routine updates can be efficiently handled via digital platforms.

The best practices in communication methods and tools in project management revolve around choosing the right medium for the message, ensuring clarity and conciseness in communication, fostering an environment of active listening, and being adaptable to different situations and needs. These practices are not just about transmitting information; they are about creating an atmosphere of openness, collaboration, and mutual understanding. In essence, effective communication is a cornerstone in the foundation of successful project management, bridging gaps, aligning visions, and steering projects towards their goals.

Overcoming Communication Barriers in Projects

Effective communication is akin to the lifeblood of a project, essential for its vitality and success. However, this flow of information is often impeded by various barriers, which, if not addressed, can lead to misunderstandings, inefficiencies, and ultimately, project failures. Overcoming these communication barriers is akin to navigating through a maze, requiring skill, patience, and a strategic approach.

One of the most common barriers in project communication is cultural and linguistic differences, especially in today's globalized work environments. Team members from different parts of the world bring diverse perspectives, languages, and communication styles. To bridge these gaps, it is essential to foster an inclusive culture that respects and acknowledges diversity. This can involve using simple, clear language, avoiding jargon and regional colloquialisms, and being mindful of cultural sensitivities. Additionally, leveraging the skills of bilingual team members or employing translation services can be instrumental in ensuring clear and accurate communication.

Another significant barrier is the physical distance in remote and distributed teams. The lack of face-to-face interaction can lead to a sense of disconnect and misinterpretations. Overcoming this challenge requires leveraging technology effectively. Utilizing video conferencing tools, collaborative platforms, and regular virtual meetings can help create a sense of proximity and connectedness. It's important to establish regular check-ins and updates, ensuring that remote team members feel as engaged and informed as those in physical office spaces.

Technological hurdles also pose a barrier to effective communication. Inadequate or complex communication tools can hinder the flow of information. The solution lies in selecting user-friendly, reliable, and accessible tools. Training and support in using these tools can also enhance communication efficiency. The key is to choose technologies that align with the project's needs and the team's comfort level.

Information overload is another common challenge. In the age of constant connectivity and data flows, team members can become overwhelmed with information, leading to confusion and disengagement. To combat this, it's crucial to streamline communication. This involves prioritizing information, ensuring messages are concise and relevant. Establishing clear communication protocols, such as defined channels for different types of information, can help in managing the flow and ensuring that important messages don't get lost in the noise.

Psychological barriers, such as personal biases, assumptions, and preconceptions, can significantly impede communication. These barriers are often subtle but can lead to a lack of understanding and trust. Overcoming these requires building a project environment based on openness, trust, and respect. Encouraging open dialogue, actively seeking feedback, and creating a safe space for expressing opinions can help in breaking down these psychological barriers.

Overcoming communication barriers in projects is crucial for the smooth execution and success of the project. It involves understanding and addressing cultural and linguistic differences, leveraging technology to bridge physical distances, managing information flow, and fostering an environment of trust and openness. By navigating these barriers with skill and empathy, project managers can ensure a free flow of information, enhancing team collaboration and steering the project toward its objectives. Effective communication is not just about exchanging information; it's about connecting people, aligning visions, and building a strong foundation for project success.

Project Communication Management Questions

1. What is the primary role of effective communication in project management?
2. How does initial communication set the foundation for a project?
3. Why is continuous communication important as a project progresses?
4. What is the significance of active listening in project communication?
5. How do communication methods and tools vary in project management?
6. What factors should be considered when choosing a communication method or tool?
7. How can cultural and linguistic differences impact project communication?
8. What strategies can be used to overcome remote and distributed team communication challenges?
9. Why is managing information overload important in project communication?
10. How can psychological barriers in communication be addressed within a project team?

Project Communication Management Answers

1. Answer: The primary role of effective communication in project management is to synchronize team efforts, align stakeholder expectations, and guide the project to successful completion, much like a conductor leading an orchestra.

2. Answer: Initial communication sets the foundation for a project by clearly articulating goals, scope, and objectives in a way that is accessible to all team members and stakeholders, ensuring everyone starts with a shared understanding.

3. Answer: Continuous communication is important as it helps navigate complexities and challenges in a project, coordinating tasks, conveying changes, resolving conflicts, and maintaining transparency and trust.

4. Answer: Active listening is significant as it allows project managers to gather valuable feedback, understand concerns, and address them promptly, ensuring a two-way communication process.

5. Answer: Communication methods and tools in project management vary from traditional face-to-face interactions to modern digital platforms like emails, instant messaging, and video conferencing, each serving unique purposes.

6. Answer: When choosing a communication method or tool, consider the nature of the information, urgency of the message, audience's preferences, and the need for documentation or real-time interaction.

7. Answer: Cultural and linguistic differences can lead to misunderstandings and misinterpretations in project communication, requiring an inclusive approach that respects diversity and possibly language translation services.

8. Answer: To overcome remote and distributed team communication challenges, leverage technology like video conferencing and collaborative platforms, establish regular check-ins, and ensure all team members feel engaged.

9. Answer: Managing information overload is important to prevent confusion and ensure that crucial messages are not lost. This involves prioritizing information, keeping messages concise, and establishing clear communication protocols.

10. Answer: Psychological barriers in communication can be addressed by building an environment based on openness, trust, and respect, encouraging open dialogue, actively seeking feedback, and creating a safe space for expressing opinions.

Chapter 10: Project Resource Management

Comprehensive Resource Management in Projects

Resource management begins with a thorough understanding of the project's scope and objectives. This foundational step is crucial, as it sets the stage for determining what resources are necessary, from personnel and equipment to materials and technology. It's a meticulous process, akin to a chef understanding the ingredients needed for a recipe. The project manager evaluates the project's requirements and identifies the resources that will bring the project to fruition. This identification process involves not just listing the resources but understanding their availability, cost, and potential constraints.

Once the resources are identified, the next step is effective allocation. This involves assigning the right resources to the right tasks at the right time. It's a delicate balancing act, ensuring that resources are utilized efficiently without over-allocation or underutilization. For example, allocating skilled team members to critical tasks while ensuring they are not spread too thin, or scheduling the use of equipment and materials to avoid bottlenecks. This strategic allocation is essential for maintaining the project's momentum and preventing delays or cost overruns.

Effective resource management also involves continuous monitoring and adaptation. Just as a captain adjusts the sails to match the wind, a project manager must be prepared to adjust resource allocation in response to project changes. This flexibility is key, as projects rarely go exactly as planned. Regular monitoring allows the project manager to identify resource-related issues early and make adjustments to keep the project on track. This monitoring involves tracking resource utilization, assessing performance, and ensuring that resources are contributing effectively to the project's goals.

Another critical aspect of comprehensive resource management is communication and collaboration. Resources, especially human resources, are not just tools to be used; they are individuals with skills, ideas, and needs. Effective communication helps in understanding these needs, aligning resources with project goals, and fostering a collaborative environment. This involves regular check-ins with team members, providing feedback, and adapting resource plans to accommodate team dynamics.

Risk management also plays a pivotal role in resource management. Risks related to resources, such as the unavailability of key personnel or delays in material delivery, can have significant impacts on the project. Proactive risk management involves identifying potential resource risks, assessing their impact, and developing mitigation strategies. This might include having contingency plans, such as backup resources or alternative sourcing strategies.

Comprehensive resource management in projects is an art that requires strategic planning, continuous monitoring, flexibility, effective communication, and proactive risk management. It's about understanding and orchestrating the various resources that a project needs, ensuring they are used efficiently and effectively.

Effective Planning and Allocation of Resources

The effective planning and allocation of resources is a delicate dance of precision and foresight. It's an art form that involves not just the identification of resources but their strategic distribution to ensure the smooth execution and successful completion of a project.

The effective resource planning begins with a deep understanding of the project's scope and objectives. This understanding is like the foundation of a building, upon which all subsequent decisions are made. The project manager assesses the project in its entirety, identifying every task and determining what resources - human, technical, financial, and material - are required. This step is crucial as it sets the tone for the resource allocation process, ensuring that the project has everything it needs to progress without interruptions.

Once the resources are identified, the next step is the strategic allocation of these resources. This stage is a balancing act, akin to an acrobat maintaining equilibrium on a tightrope. The project manager must distribute resources in a manner that optimizes their usage and aligns with the project timeline. This involves scheduling resources in a way that prevents bottlenecks while also avoiding underutilization. For instance, human resources must be allocated based on their skills and availability, ensuring that the right people are working on the right tasks at the right time. Similarly, equipment and materials must be scheduled to be available when needed, avoiding delays in project progress.

Effective resource allocation also requires a keen understanding of the project timeline and dependencies between tasks. Like threads in a tapestry, each task in a project is interconnected. The project manager must understand these interdependencies and allocate resources accordingly. This foresight ensures that resources are ready when required by subsequent tasks, maintaining a continuous flow in the project execution.

The dynamic nature of projects demands that resource planning and allocation be flexible and adaptable. Projects are prone to changes and unforeseen challenges, and the resource plan must be able to accommodate these. The project manager, therefore, must regularly review and adjust the resource allocation as the project progresses. This adaptability is like a navigator altering the course of a ship in response to changing winds and currents. It involves being proactive, anticipating potential changes, and having contingency plans in place.

Effective communication and collaboration with the project team and stakeholders are also integral to successful resource planning and allocation. The project manager must ensure that everyone involved understands the resource plan and their role in it. Regular updates and discussions help in aligning the team's efforts with the project objectives and also in identifying any issues with resource allocation that may need addressing.

Risk management plays a crucial role in the resource planning and allocation process. The project manager must consider potential risks associated with resources, such as the unavailability of key personnel or delays in resource delivery. Identifying these risks and incorporating mitigation strategies into the resource plan is essential for preventing project disruptions.

Effective planning and allocation of resources in a project is a complex process that requires strategic thinking, careful balancing, and continuous adjustment. It's about understanding the project's needs, allocating resources wisely to meet these needs, and being adaptable to changes as the project unfolds. By mastering this intricate dance of resource planning and allocation, a project manager can ensure that the project flows smoothly from start to finish, like a well-conducted symphony, each element in perfect harmony with the others.

Managing Team Resources: Development and Strategies

Managing team resources in a project is a dynamic process that resembles the careful cultivation of a garden. It's about nurturing, developing, and strategically deploying the most valuable asset of any project - its people. This process requires a blend of empathy, foresight, and tactical planning to ensure that each team member can contribute their best, grow professionally, and help drive the project towards its goals.

At the core of managing team resources is the development of the team itself. This development starts from the moment a team is formed and continues throughout the project lifecycle. Like a gardener selecting the right plants for a garden, a project manager must assemble a team with the right mix of skills, experiences, and personalities. This selection process is crucial, as it sets the tone for team dynamics and overall performance. The project manager needs to understand the strengths and weaknesses of each team member and how they complement each other, ensuring a balanced and effective team.

Once the team is in place, the focus shifts to fostering a positive and productive work environment. This involves creating an atmosphere of trust, respect, and collaboration. Like nurturing seedlings in a garden, the project manager must nurture their team, providing the support, tools, and encouragement they need to succeed. This nurturing includes regular communication, clear articulation of goals and expectations, and creating opportunities for team members to voice their ideas and concerns.

An essential strategy in managing team resources is the ongoing development and training of team members. In a rapidly evolving world, continuous learning is vital for keeping skills relevant and sharp. Like a gardener pruning and feeding plants, the project manager should provide opportunities for professional growth. This could be in the form of training sessions, workshops, or even on-the-job learning through challenging assignments. Encouraging and facilitating this growth not only enhances the team's capabilities but also boosts morale and job satisfaction.

Effective allocation of team resources is another critical aspect of team management. It's about assigning the right people to the right tasks at the right time. This allocation requires a deep understanding of each team member's skills and potential, as well as the project's requirements and timeline. Like a chess master strategically moving pieces on a board, the project manager must strategically deploy team members where they can make the most significant impact.

Adaptability is a key element in managing team resources. Projects are dynamic, and circumstances can change rapidly. The project manager must be prepared to adjust their team management strategies in response to these changes. This might involve reallocating team members to different tasks, bringing in additional resources, or even downsizing the team in response to project scope changes. This flexibility ensures that the team remains aligned with the project's evolving needs.

Recognizing and rewarding the team's efforts is crucial for maintaining motivation and morale. Acknowledging individual and team achievements, providing constructive feedback, and celebrating milestones helps in building a sense of accomplishment and belonging. It's like a gardener enjoying the beauty of the garden they've cultivated – acknowledging the team's hard work reinforces their commitment and enthusiasm for the project.

Managing team resources in a project is a multifaceted process that involves assembling the right team, nurturing a positive work environment, fostering continuous development, strategically allocating resources, being adaptable, and recognizing achievements. By effectively navigating these aspects, a project manager can harness the full potential of their team, leading to enhanced productivity, professional growth, and, ultimately, the successful realization of project goals. It's a process that requires not just managerial skills but also leadership, empathy, and strategic vision.

Conflict Resolution and Team Dynamics

Conflict resolution and managing team dynamics are akin to conducting an orchestra with diverse instruments. Each team member, with their unique personality, perspectives, and skills, contributes to the project's symphony. However, just as differing musical notes can create dissonance, so too can varying personalities and opinions lead to conflicts within a team. Skillfully managing these conflicts and understanding team dynamics are crucial for maintaining harmony and steering the project towards success.

Conflict in a team, while often perceived negatively, can be a catalyst for growth and innovation if managed effectively. It arises from differences in opinions, goals, or work methodologies. Like a knot in a thread, it needs to be untangled carefully, not cut off abruptly. The first step in resolving conflicts is to acknowledge them openly and address them promptly. Ignoring conflicts or allowing them to fester can lead to a toxic work environment, impacting team morale and project progress.

Effective conflict resolution involves understanding the root cause of the conflict. This requires active listening, empathy, and an open-minded approach from the project manager. Just as a mediator in a dialogue, the project manager must create a safe space where team members feel heard and understood. It's about encouraging open communication, where team members can express their concerns and perspectives without fear of judgment or retribution.

Once the underlying issues are identified, the next step is to explore solutions collaboratively. This process involves negotiating and finding a middle ground that aligns with the project's goals and the team's best interests. It's not about winning an argument but finding a solution that works for everyone involved. In some cases, this might involve compromise or adapting work processes to accommodate different working styles.

Another key aspect of managing team dynamics is recognizing and valuing the diversity within the team. Each team member brings a unique set of skills, experiences, and perspectives to the table. Embracing this diversity can lead to a more creative and innovative approach to problem-solving. It's about leveraging the strengths of each team member and ensuring that everyone contributes to their fullest potential.

Building trust and fostering a collaborative team environment are also essential for managing team dynamics. Trust is the foundation of any strong team, creating a sense of safety and belonging. It's built through consistency, reliability, and transparency in actions and communications. Team-building activities, regular check-ins, and celebrating team achievements can also strengthen bonds and improve team cohesion.

Continuous monitoring and adaptation are vital in managing team dynamics. Just as a project evolves, so too do team dynamics. Regularly assessing the team's health, gathering feedback, and making adjustments to team composition or work processes can help in maintaining a positive and productive work environment.

Conflict resolution and managing team dynamics are critical components of project management. They require a combination of empathy, communication skills, negotiation, and an appreciation of diversity. By effectively resolving conflicts and understanding the nuances of team dynamics, a project manager can foster a collaborative, innovative, and high-performing team. This approach not only enhances project outcomes but also contributes to a positive and fulfilling work experience for every team member.

Project Resource Management Questions

1. What is the main goal of comprehensive resource management in project management?
2. How does the project manager begin the process of resource management?
3. What is the importance of resource allocation in project management?
4. How does a project manager adapt resource allocation during a project?
5. Why is effective communication crucial in managing project resources?
6. What role does risk management play in resource management?
7. What are the first steps in effective planning and allocation of resources?

8. How does understanding team dynamics contribute to resource management?
9. Why is adaptability important in managing team resources in a project?
10. How can conflicts within a project team be effectively resolved?

Project Resource Answers

1. Answer: The main goal of comprehensive resource management in project management is to ensure the careful allocation, utilization, and optimization of all resources (personnel, equipment, materials, technology) for successful project execution.

2. Answer: The project manager begins resource management with a thorough understanding of the project's scope and objectives, followed by identifying the necessary resources and evaluating their availability and constraints.

3. Answer: Resource allocation is important as it involves strategically assigning resources to tasks, ensuring efficient utilization without over-allocation or underutilization, crucial for maintaining the project's momentum and preventing delays or cost overruns.

4. Answer: A project manager adapts resource allocation by continuously monitoring resource utilization and making necessary adjustments in response to project changes, maintaining project continuity and effectiveness.

5. Answer: Effective communication in managing project resources is crucial as it ensures understanding of resource needs, alignment with project goals, and fosters a collaborative environment among all stakeholders and team members.

6. Answer: In resource management, risk management involves identifying potential resource-related risks and developing strategies to mitigate their impact, ensuring project stability and continuity.

7. Answer: The first steps in effective planning and allocation of resources involve a deep understanding of the project's scope and objectives, followed by the strategic distribution of resources based on project requirements and timelines.

8. Answer: Understanding team dynamics is crucial in resource management as it involves leveraging individual strengths, fostering a positive work environment, and ensuring that each team member is effectively contributing to the project.

9. Answer: Adaptability in managing team resources is important as it allows for adjustments in resource allocation in response to project evolution and changing circumstances, ensuring that resources align with current project needs.

10. Answer: Conflicts within a project team can be effectively resolved by acknowledging and addressing them openly, understanding the root causes, exploring collaborative solutions, and fostering an environment of trust and open communication.

Chapter 11: Project Risk Management

Detailed Exploration of Project Risks

The concept of risk is akin to navigating through uncharted waters. Every project, irrespective of its size or scope, carries with it a spectrum of risks that, if not identified and managed proactively, can capsize even the most meticulously planned venture. A detailed exploration of project risks is not just about acknowledging their existence but delving deep into their nature, assessing their potential impact, and devising strategies to mitigate them effectively.

At the outset, it is crucial to understand that risk in a project can take various forms and originate from diverse sources. Like a storm that can emerge from any direction at sea, project risks can arise from internal processes, external factors, technological challenges, or human elements. These risks can range from budget overruns and delays to technological failures and resource shortages. The nature of these risks can vary from known risks, which can be anticipated based on past experiences or industry knowledge, to unknown risks that emerge unexpectedly during the project lifecycle.

The process of identifying these risks is the first step in a comprehensive risk management strategy. This involves not just the project manager but the entire project team, as well as stakeholders. Much like a crew on a ship keeping watch for potential obstacles, everyone involved in the project should be encouraged to identify and communicate potential risks. Tools such as brainstorming sessions, SWOT analysis (Strengths, Weaknesses, Opportunities, Threats), and expert consultations can be instrumental in uncovering risks that might not be immediately apparent.

Once the risks are identified, the next step is to assess their potential impact and likelihood. This assessment is akin to a meteorologist evaluating the potential impact of a storm – it's about understanding how severe the risk could be and the probability of its occurrence. Techniques such as qualitative and quantitative risk analysis are employed to gauge the severity and likelihood of each identified risk. This analysis helps in prioritizing risks, focusing attention and resources on those that pose the greatest threat to the project's success.

The heart of risk management lies in developing and implementing strategies to mitigate these risks. This involves a range of tactics, from avoiding or transferring the risk to accepting or mitigating it. Like a captain charting a course away from a storm, the project manager develops strategies to navigate around high-risk scenarios or reduce their impact. This could involve contingency planning, securing insurance, adjusting project plans, or building buffers into project schedules and budgets.

Monitoring and controlling risks is an ongoing process in project management. As a project progresses, new risks may emerge, and existing risks may evolve. Regular risk reviews, continuous monitoring, and being adaptable to implement risk response plans are essential aspects of effective risk management. This continuous vigilance ensures that the project remains on course, even in the face of unforeseen challenges.

A detailed exploration of project risks is a critical component of successful project management. It involves identifying, assessing, prioritizing, and mitigating risks in a proactive manner. Effective risk management is not just about preventing negative outcomes; it's about ensuring the smooth sailing of the project through uncertain waters, prepared to face and overcome challenges that may arise along the journey. By adeptly managing risks, project managers can not only safeguard their projects but also seize opportunities that arise from these challenges, steering their projects towards successful completion.

Advanced Techniques in Risk Identification and Analysis

The identification and analysis of risks are critical movements that define the performance's success. These steps are not just precautionary measures but essential strategies that empower project managers to anticipate challenges and prepare effectively.

It's akin to a detective meticulously searching for clues, delving into every aspect of the project to uncover potential risks. This process involves a combination of methods, each offering a unique lens through which risks can be identified. One such method is the Delphi Technique, which involves consulting with experts and synthesizing their insights to identify risks that might not be evident to the project team. This technique taps into a wealth of experience and expertise, bringing to light risks that are less obvious but potentially impactful.

Another innovative method is scenario analysis, a technique that involves creating detailed narratives of possible future events. Much like an author crafting different storylines, the project manager explores various scenarios, considering how different conditions and decisions might affect the project's outcome. This technique helps in visualizing risks in different contexts and preparing for a range of possible futures.

Once risks are identified, the next stage is analysis, which involves assessing the likelihood and impact of each risk. Advanced techniques in this realm go beyond simple estimations, employing quantitative methods to provide a more objective analysis. Monte Carlo simulations, for instance, use computer algorithms to simulate thousands of scenarios, providing a statistical distribution of possible outcomes. This technique offers a sophisticated way to quantify risk, turning abstract uncertainties into concrete data.

Risk mapping, or risk matrix, is another valuable tool in risk analysis. It's a visual representation that plots risks based on their likelihood and impact, creating a clear overview of the risk landscape. This map helps in prioritizing risks, focusing attention on those that are both likely to occur and have significant consequences. It's like a navigation chart for a ship's captain, highlighting the areas that require the most attention and careful navigation.

Furthermore, the integration of risk identification and analysis into the overall project management process is crucial. This integration ensures that risk management is not an isolated activity but a continuous thread that runs through the project's lifecycle. It involves embedding risk considerations into decision-making processes, from initial planning to execution and closure. Regular risk reviews and updates ensure that the risk management strategy remains relevant and effective as the project evolves.

Effective communication also plays a pivotal role in advanced risk management. It involves not just documenting risks but sharing this information with the team and stakeholders in a clear and understandable manner. It's about creating a culture of open discussion around risks, where team members feel empowered to voice concerns and share insights.

Advanced techniques in risk identification and analysis are essential components of sophisticated project management. They involve a blend of expert consultation, scenario planning, quantitative analysis, risk mapping, and continuous integration of risk management into the project process. By employing these techniques, project managers can gain a deep and nuanced understanding of potential risks, prepare effectively for them, and steer their projects towards successful completion, even in the face of uncertainties and challenges.

Innovative Approaches to Planning Risk Responses and Controls

Planning risk responses and controls is akin to charting a course through uncharted waters. The traditional methods of risk management, while foundational, are increasingly being complemented by innovative approaches that offer enhanced flexibility and effectiveness. These contemporary strategies are like navigational aids, helping project managers to not only anticipate and respond to risks but also to harness them for project success.

One innovative approach in planning risk responses is the adoption of Agile methodologies. Traditionally associated with software development, Agile's principles are now being applied to risk management in various project types. Agile risk management involves iterative planning and regular reassessment of risks, allowing teams to respond quickly to changes. This approach is particularly effective in projects where risks are high and change rapidly. It involves breaking down the project into smaller segments or sprints, each with its own risk assessment and response planning. This method allows for more frequent adjustments and a continuous focus on risk, ensuring that the project can adapt swiftly to new challenges as they arise.

Another cutting-edge strategy is the use of big data and predictive analytics in risk planning. By harnessing the power of vast amounts of data and advanced analytical tools, project managers can predict potential risks with greater accuracy. This technique involves analyzing historical data, market trends, and other relevant information to identify patterns and predict future risks. Predictive analytics can provide insights into the likelihood of certain risks occurring and their potential impact, enabling project managers to prepare more targeted and effective response strategies.

Risk visualization tools represent another innovative trend in risk management. These tools use graphical representations to map out risks and their interconnections. This visualization aids in understanding the complexity of the risk landscape and in communicating risks to stakeholders more effectively. Tools like risk heat maps or risk interconnection diagrams can help in identifying which risks have the most significant impact and should be prioritized in response planning.

Collaborative risk management is also gaining traction as an innovative approach. This strategy involves engaging all project stakeholders in the risk management process. By involving team members, clients, suppliers, and other stakeholders in identifying and planning for risks, a project can benefit from a broader range of perspectives and expertise. This collaborative approach can lead to more comprehensive risk identification and more robust and creative risk response strategies.

Additionally, the integration of risk management with project learning and continuous improvement is an innovative concept that adds value to the entire project management process. This approach involves using the insights gained from managing risks to improve project processes and methodologies. Lessons learned from handling risks are documented and shared, helping to prevent similar issues in future projects and contributing to the development of best practices in risk management.

Innovative approaches to planning risk responses and controls in project management involve the application of Agile principles, the use of big data and predictive analytics, risk visualization tools, collaborative risk management, and the integration of risk management with project learning. These strategies offer a more dynamic, data-driven, and collaborative approach to risk management, enabling project managers to navigate through uncertainties more effectively. By embracing these innovative approaches, project managers can not only mitigate risks more effectively but also turn them into opportunities for project enhancement and success.

Real-life Risk Management Scenarios and Solutions

Risk management is often where theory meets reality. Real-life risk management scenarios are like unpredictable plot twists in a well-planned story, challenging project managers to adapt their strategies and find innovative solutions. Exploring some of these scenarios and the solutions applied provides valuable insights into the practicalities of risk management in dynamic project environments.

For instance, a major construction project might encounter unexpected geological challenges, leading to significant delays. In such a situation, proactive risk management involves first acknowledging the problem and then reevaluating the project timeline and resources. The project manager, in this case, might negotiate with stakeholders to extend deadlines, allocate additional resources to expedite the work, or even redesign certain aspects of the project to accommodate the unexpected conditions. This approach not only addresses the immediate problem but also sets a precedent for handling similar issues in the future.

Another scenario often encountered is budget overruns, especially in technology projects where scope creep is common. A software development project, for example, might see its scope gradually expanding as stakeholders request additional features. This can lead to budget overruns if not managed effectively. An effective solution in this scenario is implementing strict change control processes. The project manager would assess the impact of each requested change on the project's budget and timeline, and then make informed decisions about which changes to implement. Regular communication with stakeholders about the implications of scope changes on budget and time can also help manage expectations and mitigate this risk.

In the realm of event management, one might encounter the risk of poor attendance. For instance, an organization planning a major conference might face the risk of lower-than-expected attendance due to various factors like competing events or economic downturns. To mitigate this risk, the project manager could employ strategies such as diversifying the marketing channels, offering early bird discounts, or providing virtual attendance options. These solutions aim to increase the event's appeal and accessibility, thus boosting attendance.

Supply chain disruptions are another common risk, particularly in manufacturing projects. A company reliant on components from various global suppliers might face delays due to geopolitical issues or transportation disruptions. To mitigate this risk, the project manager might develop a diversified supplier strategy, maintaining relationships with multiple suppliers to ensure a steady supply chain. Additionally, maintaining a buffer stock of critical components can also be an effective strategy to minimize the impact of supply chain disruptions.

In a technology project, a significant risk is often technological failure or cybersecurity threats. For example, a company implementing a new IT system may face risks related to system compatibility or data breaches. To address these risks, the project manager would work closely with IT specialists to conduct thorough system testing and implement robust cybersecurity measures. Regular updates and maintenance, along with employee training on cybersecurity best practices, can further mitigate these risks.

Real-life risk management scenarios require project managers to apply their knowledge and skills in dynamic and often challenging situations. The solutions to these risks involve a combination of strategic planning, effective communication, and adaptability. These scenarios underscore the importance of proactive risk identification and assessment, as well as the need for flexible and innovative problem-solving approaches. By effectively navigating these risks, project managers can guide their projects through uncertainties and ensure their successful completion.

Project Risk Management Questions

1. What is the primary goal of risk management in project management?
2. Can you list the different types of sources from which risks can arise in a project?
3. Describe the initial step in a comprehensive risk management strategy.
4. How does the Delphi Technique aid in risk identification?
5. What role does quantitative analysis play in risk assessment?
6. Explain how Agile methodologies can be applied in risk management.
7. How do big data and predictive analytics contribute to risk management?
8. What are some common real-life scenarios of risk in project management?
9. How can a project manager deal with the risk of project delays due to unexpected issues?
10. What is the significance of adaptable strategies in the context of risk management?

Project Risk Management Answers

1. Answer: The primary goal of risk management in project management is to proactively identify, assess, and mitigate potential challenges to ensure the project's success.

2. Answer: Risks in a project can arise from various sources such as internal processes, external factors, technological challenges, or human elements.

3. Answer: The initial step in risk management is the process of risk identification, involving the entire project team and stakeholders to uncover potential risks.

4. Answer: The Delphi Technique involves consulting with experts to synthesize their insights, helping to identify risks that might not be evident to the project team.

5. Answer: Quantitative analysis in risk assessment involves using statistical methods to gauge the severity and likelihood of risks, aiding in prioritizing them.

6. Answer: Agile methodologies in risk management involve iterative planning and regular reassessment of risks, allowing teams to respond quickly to changes.

7. Answer: Big data and predictive analytics help in risk management by analyzing historical data, market trends, and other relevant information to identify patterns and predict future risks.

8. Answer: Common real-life scenarios of risk include project delays, budget overruns, supply chain disruptions, and technological failures.

9. Answer: To deal with project delays, a project manager might reevaluate the timeline and resources, negotiate deadline extensions, or redesign certain project aspects.

10. Answer: Adaptable strategies in risk management are crucial as they allow project managers to adjust their plans and strategies in response to changing conditions and unforeseen challenges.

Chapter 12: Project Stakeholder Management

Stakeholder Identification and Analysis: In-depth Approach

Stakeholders are the individual pieces whose interests, expectations, and involvement are crucial to the project's overall picture. Effective stakeholder identification and analysis is an in-depth process, requiring a nuanced understanding of all the parties involved in or affected by the project. This approach is akin to a detective meticulously piecing together clues to understand the broader narrative.

The process begins with broad stakeholder identification. This stage is like casting a wide net to capture every individual, group, or organization that could potentially influence or be influenced by the project. Stakeholders can range from direct actors like team members, customers, and suppliers to more indirect influencers such as regulatory bodies, community groups, or even the media. This comprehensive gathering of stakeholders is vital because overlooking even a single entity can lead to unforeseen complications later in the project.

The next step involves delving deeper into understanding their specific interests, expectations, and the degree of influence they hold over the project. This analysis is much like a sculptor chiseling away at a block of stone to reveal the intricate forms beneath. Various tools and techniques, such as stakeholder mapping or analysis matrices, can be employed here. These tools help categorize stakeholders based on their level of interest and influence, providing a clear picture of who needs the most attention and management.

A key aspect of in-depth stakeholder analysis is recognizing that stakeholders are not static entities; their levels of interest and influence can change over the course of the project. For instance, a regulatory body might have a low interest in the project initially but could become highly influential if compliance issues arise. Similarly, community groups might become more interested as the project progresses and its impacts become more apparent. This dynamic nature of stakeholders necessitates regular reassessment and adjustment of the stakeholder management strategy.

Effective stakeholder analysis also involves understanding the relationships and networks between different stakeholders. In many projects, stakeholders are interlinked in complex ways, and the actions of one can significantly impact others. Understanding these networks is crucial for anticipating reactions and managing stakeholder interactions effectively. This understanding helps in creating strategies that not only address individual stakeholder needs but also manage the interplay between different groups.

Once the analysis is complete, the insights gained become the foundation for developing a comprehensive stakeholder engagement and communication plan. This plan outlines how and when stakeholders will be engaged and communicated with throughout the project. It considers the various interests and levels of influence, tailoring the communication strategy to ensure that all stakeholders are kept informed and involved in a manner that is appropriate to their role in the project.

Stakeholder identification and analysis is a critical and in-depth process in project management. It involves a thorough understanding of all parties involved, assessing their interests and influences, and continually adapting to their evolving dynamics. This process is not just a preliminary step in project planning; it's an ongoing strategy that ensures all voices are heard and considered, thus paving the way for a smoother project journey and a more successful outcome. By meticulously analyzing and engaging with stakeholders, project managers can build strong relationships, mitigate risks, and harness stakeholder contributions to enhance the project's success.

Engagement Strategies for Stakeholders

Engaging stakeholders is akin to conducting an orchestra where each musician plays a crucial part in the symphony's success. Stakeholder engagement is not just about informing people; it's about building relationships, fostering trust, and ensuring that those who have a stake in the project are actively involved and supportive. Developing and implementing effective engagement strategies is crucial in navigating the complexities of diverse interests and expectations.

The first step in crafting engagement strategies is understanding the stakeholders. This understanding goes beyond simply identifying who they are; it involves delving into their interests, concerns, influence, and expectations from the project. Like a psychologist understanding their patient, a project manager must understand what motivates stakeholders, what they value, and how the project impacts them. This depth of understanding is crucial in tailoring the engagement approach to suit each stakeholder's unique profile.

Once stakeholders are understood, the next step is to develop a communication plan that is as diverse as the stakeholders themselves. This plan should outline how and when stakeholders will be communicated with, taking into consideration their preferences and needs. For some, regular detailed reports might be necessary, while others might prefer brief, high-level updates. For instance, team members might need daily briefings, whereas investors might require weekly progress reports. The communication should be clear, concise, and tailored to convey the right message to the right audience in the right way.

Another key strategy is involving stakeholders in the planning and decision-making processes. This involvement can range from consulting them during the initial stages of the project to involving them in key decisions. This inclusive approach not only provides valuable insights but also fosters a sense of ownership among stakeholders, increasing their commitment to the project's success. It's like inviting guests to contribute to a meal's preparation – it enhances their experience and investment in the event.

Adapting to stakeholders' feedback is also a vital part of engagement. Engagement is a two-way process, and stakeholders often provide feedback, concerns, and ideas that can be invaluable to the project. Actively listening and responding to this feedback demonstrates respect and consideration for their input. This adaptive approach can lead to improvements in project processes and outcomes and can also prevent potential issues from escalating.

Recognizing and managing stakeholder expectations is another crucial aspect of engagement. Expectations can vary widely, and not all may be realistic or aligned with the project's objectives. Managing these expectations involves clear communication about what is feasible, negotiating compromises where necessary, and setting realistic and achievable goals. This management prevents disappointment and dissatisfaction, which can adversely affect the project.

Building and maintaining trust with stakeholders throughout the project lifecycle is essential. Trust is the foundation of effective engagement. It is built through consistent, honest communication, reliability in meeting commitments, and transparency in operations. Trust makes difficult conversations easier and enhances cooperation and support from stakeholders.

Engagement strategies for stakeholders are vital in ensuring the smooth execution and success of a project. These strategies involve understanding stakeholders, developing tailored communication plans, involving them in the project, adapting to their feedback, managing their expectations, and building trust. By effectively engaging stakeholders, a project manager can not only navigate the complexities of diverse interests and expectations but also harness the collective support, insights, and contributions of all those involved, leading to a more successful and well-rounded project outcome.

Managing Stakeholder Expectations: Advanced Techniques

Advanced techniques in managing stakeholder expectations start with an in-depth stakeholder analysis. This analysis goes beyond identifying who the stakeholders are, delving into their motivations, concerns, and how the project impacts them. Like a psychologist piecing together a client's thought patterns, a project manager uses tools like stakeholder interviews, surveys, and SWOT analyses (Strengths, Weaknesses, Opportunities, Threats) to gain a deeper understanding. This comprehensive understanding forms the basis for developing tailored strategies to manage each stakeholder's expectations effectively.

Effective communication is the cornerstone of managing stakeholder expectations. This communication must be clear, consistent, and tailored to the audience. Advanced techniques include using storytelling and visualization to convey complex project details in a more digestible and engaging manner. For example, rather than presenting stakeholders with dense reports, a project manager might use infographics or dashboards that provide a quick, visual summary of the project's status. This approach not only makes the information more accessible but also more memorable.

Setting realistic and clear expectations from the outset is another critical technique. This involves transparent discussions about the project's scope, deliverables, timelines, and potential risks. The project manager must ensure that stakeholders have a realistic understanding of what can be achieved, balancing optimism with pragmatism. Setting these expectations is not a one-time event; it involves regular revisiting and adjustment as the project progresses.

Proactive engagement is key in managing stakeholder expectations. Rather than waiting for stakeholders to raise concerns, advanced strategies involve regularly seeking their input and feedback. This could be through structured meetings, informal check-ins, or collaborative workshops. By actively involving stakeholders in the project's planning and decision-making processes, they become more invested in the project's success and more understanding of the challenges encountered along the way.

Empathy plays a significant role in managing expectations. Understanding the stakeholder's viewpoint, acknowledging their concerns, and showing that their input is valued can go a long way in maintaining positive relationships. Techniques such as active listening and empathetic communication help in building trust and rapport with stakeholders.

Another advanced technique is flexibility in managing expectations. Projects are dynamic, with changes and unforeseen events being a common occurrence. The project manager must be adept at adjusting strategies in response to these changes and effectively communicating these adjustments to stakeholders. This flexibility helps in managing stakeholder expectations in a way that aligns with the evolving nature of the project.

Managing stakeholder expectations in a project involves a sophisticated mix of in-depth analysis, effective communication, proactive engagement, empathy, and flexibility. These advanced techniques are essential for ensuring that stakeholders' expectations are aligned with the project's realities, helping to foster a supportive and collaborative environment. By skillfully managing expectations, a project manager can navigate the complexities of stakeholder relationships, mitigating risks of dissatisfaction and conflict, and steering the project towards a successful conclusion that meets the needs and expectations of all involved parties.

Case Studies in Stakeholder Management

Stakeholder management is a pivotal aspect of project management, often illustrated vividly through real-life case studies. These case studies not only highlight the complexities of managing diverse stakeholder groups but also offer valuable lessons in balancing varied interests and expectations.

1. In the context of stakeholder management, a significant case from the construction industry demonstrates the power of effective stakeholder engagement. A substantial infrastructure project in a busy city brought together a diverse array of stakeholders, including the construction company, local government, investors, residents, and environmental groups. Initially, the project was met with considerable resistance from local residents and environmentalists, who were deeply concerned about its potential impact on the community and environment.

   The pivotal shift occurred when the project managers embraced a more inclusive stakeholder management strategy. Recognizing the importance of these stakeholders' concerns, they initiated a series of community meetings. These meetings were not mere formalities; they were genuine forums for listening to and understanding the residents' apprehensions. Additionally, the project team engaged proactively with environmental groups. These discussions were centered on exploring and implementing sustainable practices that would mitigate environmental impacts.

   Collaboration with local authorities was also intensified to ensure full compliance with all relevant regulations. This multifaceted approach to stakeholder management transformed the project's trajectory. By actively including key stakeholders in the decision-making process and earnestly addressing their concerns, the project team was able to significantly reduce opposition. This strategy not only facilitated smoother project progress but also established a broader base of support, showcasing the effectiveness of thorough and thoughtful stakeholder engagement in overcoming challenges and fostering project success.

2. In the technology sector, a case study demonstrates the importance of stakeholder management during a software product launch. A tech company, expecting high demand, released a new software product. However, the launch was met with mixed reviews, as key customers expressed dissatisfaction. This feedback highlighted a critical oversight in the development process: key customers were not sufficiently involved, leading to a disconnect between their expectations and the product delivered.

   Recognizing this gap, the company's project team took immediate action to realign with their stakeholders' needs. They established a customer advisory board, a strategic move to bring key clients into the fold of the product development cycle. This board served as a platform for ongoing dialogue, allowing customers to voice their feedback and concerns directly.

   The formation of the advisory board marked a pivotal shift in the company's approach to stakeholder engagement. It enabled the company to tailor the product more closely to its customers' needs and preferences. This collaborative process involved customers in refining and enhancing the product, aligning it more closely with their expectations.

   This strategy yielded multiple benefits. It led to tangible improvements in the software, guided by direct input from its primary users. Additionally, it fostered stronger relationships with key stakeholders. By involving them in the process, the company demonstrated a commitment to listening to and valuing their input, which in turn enhanced customer loyalty and satisfaction.

This case study illustrates the critical role of stakeholder engagement in product development, particularly in the technology sector. It shows that involving key stakeholders, especially customers, is not just beneficial for product enhancement but is also essential for building trust and loyalty. The company's responsive and inclusive approach to stakeholder management turned initial criticism into an opportunity for growth and relationship building, ultimately contributing to the product's and the company's success.

3. The renovation of a hospital in the healthcare sector offers a vital case study in managing diverse stakeholder expectations effectively. The project team, tasked with a major renovation, faced the intricate challenge of aligning the interests and expectations of various stakeholders, including hospital staff, patients, regulatory bodies, and the local community.

    Recognizing the complexity of this task, the project team prioritized establishing robust and clear communication channels. This strategy was aimed at keeping all parties informed about the renovation's progress and addressing how each stakeholder group would benefit from the upgrades. For instance, staff members were updated on how the renovation would improve their working conditions, while patients were informed about enhanced healthcare facilities and services.

    In addition to regular updates, the project team implemented a feedback mechanism. This system was crucial for identifying and addressing concerns in a timely manner, allowing stakeholders to voice their opinions and feel heard. The feedback mechanism was a pivotal tool in maintaining an open dialogue between the project team and the stakeholders, fostering a sense of involvement and partnership.

    The emphasis on transparent and continuous communication proved highly effective. It enabled the hospital to navigate the renovation process with minimal disruption to its critical services. More importantly, it ensured a high level of satisfaction among all stakeholders. Keeping them informed and engaged helped mitigate potential frustrations and opposition, smoothing the path for the project's successful completion.

    This case study underscores the significance of proactive stakeholder management in complex projects within the healthcare sector. It demonstrates how effective communication and a responsive feedback system can align and fulfill the varied expectations of different stakeholder groups. By doing so, the project team not only ensured the smooth execution of the renovation but also bolstered the overall support and satisfaction of those directly and indirectly impacted by the project.

4. In the context of a multinational corporation implementing an enterprise-wide software system, we encounter a vivid example of the crucial role stakeholder management plays in organizational change. Initially, the project team faced substantial resistance from employees who were deeply entrenched in the routines of the existing system. This resistance posed a significant barrier to the successful adoption of the new software.

    Recognizing the critical need to address this challenge, the project team shifted their focus towards more intensive change management strategies. Central to this revised approach was the development and implementation of comprehensive training programs. These programs were designed not just to familiarize employees with the new system but also to highlight its benefits and efficiencies compared to the old system.

In addition to training, the project team established open forums. These forums served as platforms for employees to voice their concerns and reservations about the new software. By providing a space for open dialogue, the project team could directly address employee concerns, alleviate misconceptions, and gather valuable feedback to refine the implementation process.

Another strategic move was to actively involve employees in the rollout process of the new system. This involvement ranged from participating in pilot programs to providing input on user interface design and functionality. Engaging employees in this manner helped foster a sense of ownership and involvement in the change process, thereby reducing resistance.

The impact of these change management strategies was profound. The initial resistance from employees gradually diminished as they became more familiar and comfortable with the new system. The comprehensive training, open forums for discussion, and direct involvement in the rollout process not only eased the transition but also facilitated a more effective and smoother adoption of the software across the corporation.

This case study underscores the importance of stakeholder management, particularly in the context of organizational change. It demonstrates that effective stakeholder engagement, through training, open communication, and active involvement, is key to overcoming resistance and ensuring the successful implementation of new systems or processes within an organization. By adopting a stakeholder-centric approach, the multinational corporation was able to navigate the challenges of change management and achieve a successful transition to the new software system.

These case studies in stakeholder management demonstrate the importance of understanding and addressing the needs and concerns of all stakeholder groups involved in a project. They underscore the need for effective communication, inclusive decision-making, empathy, and adaptability in stakeholder management strategies. By prioritizing stakeholder engagement and addressing their concerns, projects can not only avoid conflicts and delays but also enhance their chances of success and acceptance.

Project Stakeholder Management Questions

1. What is the primary purpose of stakeholder identification and analysis in project management?
2. Describe the initial steps involved in effective stakeholder management.
3. How can stakeholder mapping or analysis matrices aid in managing stakeholders?
4. Why is it important to recognize the dynamic nature of stakeholders in a project?
5. How does understanding stakeholder relationships and networks benefit a project manager?
6. What role does communication play in stakeholder engagement and management?
7. Explain the significance of adapting stakeholder engagement strategies over the course of a project.
8. How can proactive engagement with stakeholders benefit a project?
9. Discuss the importance of managing stakeholder expectations in project management.
10. Give an example of a real-life scenario where effective stakeholder management was crucial to a project's success.

Project Stakeholder Management Answers

1. Answer: The primary purpose of stakeholder identification and analysis is to understand all parties involved or affected by the project, assess their interests and influence, and develop strategies to effectively engage and manage them throughout the project lifecycle.

2. Answer: The initial steps in effective stakeholder management involve identifying all potential stakeholders and then analyzing their specific interests, expectations, and the degree of influence they hold over the project.

3. Answer: Stakeholder mapping or analysis matrices help categorize stakeholders based on their level of interest and influence, providing a clear picture of who needs the most attention and management, and aiding in prioritization.

4. Answer: Recognizing the dynamic nature of stakeholders is important because their levels of interest and influence can change as the project progresses, necessitating regular reassessment and adjustment of the stakeholder management strategy.

5. Answer: Understanding stakeholder relationships and networks helps anticipate reactions and manage interactions effectively, as it reveals how actions of one stakeholder can impact others.

6. Answer: Communication is essential in stakeholder engagement and management as it ensures all stakeholders are kept informed and involved in a manner that is appropriate to their role in the project. It fosters a collaborative environment and helps in aligning the stakeholders with the project goals.

7. Answer: Adapting stakeholder engagement strategies is significant as it ensures that the approach remains effective in the face of changing project dynamics and evolving stakeholder interests and needs.

8. Answer: Proactive engagement with stakeholders involves regularly seeking their input and feedback, which can provide valuable insights, foster a sense of ownership, increase their commitment to the project, and help in anticipating and addressing potential issues.

9. Answer: Managing stakeholder expectations is crucial as it involves setting realistic and achievable goals, communicating clearly about what is feasible, and negotiating compromises where necessary, thus preventing disappointment and dissatisfaction.

10. Answer: An example of effective stakeholder management is seen in a large infrastructure project in a city, where initial opposition from local residents and environmentalists was mitigated by the project managers adopting a more inclusive approach, engaging these groups in discussions, and addressing their concerns.

Chapter 13: Project Procurement Management

Procurement Processes in Project Management

The procurement process begins with thorough planning, which lays the foundation for effective procurement activities. This initial step is akin to a cartographer mapping out a route; it involves identifying the project's needs in terms of materials, equipment, and services. The project manager must understand the project's objectives, timelines, and constraints to develop a procurement plan that aligns with the overall project strategy. This plan outlines what needs to be procured, when, and how, setting the stage for the subsequent steps in the procurement process.

Following the planning phase, the next critical step is the selection process. This step involves identifying potential suppliers and evaluating them based on criteria such as cost, quality, reliability, and service. It's like auditioning actors for a play; the project manager must choose the best candidates who can deliver outstanding performances. The selection process often involves soliciting bids or proposals from various suppliers, a methodical evaluation of these bids, and then selecting the supplier that offers the best value for the project.

Negotiation is another key element of the procurement process. Once a supplier is selected, the project manager enters into negotiations to finalize the terms of the contract. This negotiation is not just about price but also about terms and conditions, delivery schedules, quality standards, and payment terms. It's a delicate balancing act, much like a diplomat negotiating a treaty, where the project manager must strike a deal that meets the project's needs while ensuring a fair arrangement for both parties.

Effective procurement also involves rigorous contract management. After the contract is signed, the project manager must ensure that the supplier delivers as per the agreement. This involves monitoring the supplier's performance, managing the relationship, and handling any issues that arise. It's like a stage manager ensuring that every element of a production is executed flawlessly. This phase ensures that the goods or services procured meet the specified requirements and are delivered on time and within budget.

Finally, the procurement process in project management is not complete without proper closure. This involves evaluating the supplier's performance, making any final payments, and documenting lessons learned for future projects. This closure is akin to the final act of a play, where the outcomes are assessed, and the stage is set for future performances.

In conclusion, procurement processes in project management are a complex blend of planning, selection, negotiation, management, and closure. These processes are critical to ensuring that the project has access to the necessary resources at the right time and price, and of the desired quality. By effectively managing these processes, a project manager can significantly contribute to the project's success, ensuring that it is not only completed within its constraints but also meets or exceeds its objectives.

Effective Planning and Execution of Procurements

The planning and execution of procurements is a critical endeavor that can significantly influence a project's trajectory. This complex process requires a strategic and methodical approach, akin to a chess grandmaster devising and executing a meticulous plan. Effective procurement planning and execution are not merely about acquiring goods and services; they are about ensuring these acquisitions align perfectly with the project's objectives, timelines, and budget constraints.

The journey of effective procurement begins with meticulous planning. This phase is the bedrock upon which successful procurement activities are built, much like an architect drafting a detailed blueprint before construction. In this planning stage, the project manager must first identify all the project's procurement needs. This identification involves a thorough analysis of the project scope, schedule, and resources, determining precisely what needs to be procured, in what quantities, and when. It's a process that requires not only a deep understanding of the project itself but also of the market landscape from which these resources will be sourced.

Once the procurement needs are identified, the next critical step is developing a comprehensive procurement plan. This plan is a strategic document that outlines how the procurement process will be conducted. It covers aspects such as the method of procurement (e.g., tendering, direct purchase), criteria for supplier selection, risk management strategies, and timelines for procurement activities. This plan acts as a roadmap, guiding the project team through the procurement process, ensuring that each step is thoughtfully considered and aligned with the project's overall strategy.

The execution of procurements is where the plan is put into action. This stage is a ballet of coordination and precision, involving issuing requests for proposals (RFPs), evaluating bids, negotiating contracts, and managing suppliers. Each step must be executed with attention to detail and adherence to the procurement plan. The evaluation of bids, for instance, is not just about looking at the price; it's about assessing the overall value that each supplier brings, considering factors such as quality, reliability, and compliance with project requirements.

Negotiation is a pivotal part of the execution phase. In this, the project manager must possess a blend of diplomacy and assertiveness. Negotiations are not solely focused on price but also encompass terms and conditions, delivery schedules, and after-sales service. The goal is to arrive at a mutually beneficial agreement that ensures the project receives the right quality of goods or services within the necessary timeframe and at a reasonable cost.

Effective procurement also involves rigorous contract management. This management extends beyond just signing a contract; it encompasses overseeing the supplier's performance throughout the project lifecycle. Regular monitoring, communication with suppliers, and addressing any issues promptly are essential components of effective contract management. It ensures that the supplier upholds their end of the bargain and any deviations are rectified swiftly to avoid impacting the project adversely.

The final stage of procurement is the closure. This involves reviewing supplier performance, making final payments, and documenting any lessons learned. This stage is crucial for continuous improvement, allowing the project team to refine their procurement processes for future projects.

Effective planning and execution of procurements in project management require a comprehensive and strategic approach. From meticulous planning to careful execution and thorough contract management, each step is vital in ensuring that the procurements align with and support the project's goals. By skillfully navigating these steps, project managers can ensure that their projects are equipped with the necessary resources to succeed, delivered in a timely, cost-effective, and quality-assured manner.

Understanding and Managing Contract Types and Relationships

Each contract, with its unique terms, conditions, and obligations, represents a distinct relationship between parties, requiring meticulous management to ensure mutual benefit and project success. Understanding and managing contract types and relationships is akin to navigating the complex web of international diplomacy. This intricate process demands not only a deep understanding of different contract types but also the skill to manage the relationships they embody.

At the heart of this endeavor is the recognition of the various contract types commonly used in projects, each tailored to different risk profiles and project requirements. Fixed-price contracts, for instance, offer a single set price for all work performed, transferring the risk of cost overruns from the buyer to the seller. This type of contract is akin to a well-defined treaty, where terms are clear, but flexibility is limited. It's favored in projects with well-defined scopes where costs can be accurately estimated upfront.

On the other end of the spectrum are cost-reimbursable contracts, which cover the actual costs of the work plus an additional fee for profit. This contract type is more like an open agreement that allows for adjustments along the way, suitable for projects where the scope is not fully defined at the outset. The flexibility it offers comes with a shared risk, requiring trust and transparency between parties to manage costs effectively.

Time and materials contracts represent a hybrid of the two, allowing for payment based on the actual cost of materials and labor rates. This type of contract is comparable to an alliance that adjusts to circumstances, providing flexibility while attempting to keep an eye on costs. It's often used when it's clear that work is needed but the extent of the work is not known.

Understanding these contract types is crucial, but it's just the beginning. Managing the relationships these contracts represent requires a blend of communication, negotiation, and oversight skills. Effective communication is the cornerstone, ensuring that all parties have a clear understanding of the contract terms, expectations, and any changes that occur. Regular updates, meetings, and transparent documentation form the basis of a strong contractual relationship.

Negotiation is another critical aspect of managing contract types and relationships. Before entering into a contract, negotiation sets the stage for a fair and mutually beneficial agreement. This involves not just discussing costs and deliverables but also negotiating terms that protect all parties' interests, such as clauses for change management, dispute resolution, and termination.

Once a contract is in place, diligent oversight is essential to ensure compliance with its terms. This involves monitoring performance, managing changes, and addressing any issues promptly. It's a process that requires a keen eye for detail and the ability to maintain a strong partnership with the contractor, balancing firmness with flexibility.

Moreover, managing contract relationships also involves preparing for and managing risks. Understanding the potential risks associated with each type of contract and having strategies in place to mitigate these risks is vital. This could involve setting up escrow accounts for fixed-price contracts, conducting regular audits for cost-reimbursable contracts, or establishing clear benchmarks for time and materials contracts.

In conclusion, understanding and managing contract types and relationships is a critical competency in project management. It requires a deep understanding of the various contract types, the ability to negotiate terms that align with project goals, and the skills to manage the relationships and risks these contracts entail. By navigating these aspects with care and precision, project managers can ensure that contractual relationships contribute positively to the project's outcomes, fostering cooperation and success across the board.

Ethical Considerations in Procurement Management

Each decision and action must be balanced with integrity to ensure fairness, transparency, and accountability. Ethical considerations in procurement management are paramount, as these practices not only reflect the moral compass of the organization but also significantly impact its reputation, relationships, and success.

At the core of ethical procurement management lies the principle of fairness. This principle is about providing equal opportunities for all potential suppliers and vendors. It's akin to holding an open audition where every actor gets a chance to perform. Fairness ensures that the procurement process is competitive and unbiased, allowing the best supplier to be selected based on merit rather than favoritism or nepotism. This approach fosters a culture of integrity and trust, which is crucial for long-term relationships with suppliers.

Transparency is another critical ethical consideration. Like a glass house that hides nothing, the procurement process should be open and clear to all stakeholders. Transparency involves sharing procurement criteria, processes, and decisions openly, ensuring that all actions are visible and justifiable. This openness not only builds trust among suppliers but also among internal stakeholders and the public, reinforcing the organization's commitment to ethical practices.

Accountability in procurement management is about taking responsibility for decisions and their outcomes. It's the assurance that procurement activities are conducted according to established policies and laws, and that there is a mechanism in place to address any discrepancies or grievances. Like a captain who stands by the ship's wheel, procurement managers must ensure that they, along with their teams, adhere to ethical standards and are prepared to answer for their actions. This responsibility underscores the importance of ethical decision-making and the role of procurement managers in upholding these values.

Conflict of interest is a significant ethical challenge in procurement management. It occurs when personal interests collide with professional duties, potentially influencing decision-making. Managing this challenge requires strict policies and procedures to identify and mitigate conflicts of interest. For instance, employees involved in procurement should disclose any potential conflicts, and in cases where conflicts are identified, those individuals should be recused from the decision-making process. Addressing conflicts of interest with rigor and transparency is essential to maintaining the integrity of the procurement process.

Sustainability and social responsibility have also emerged as vital ethical considerations. Ethical procurement goes beyond economic factors to include environmental and social impacts. This broader perspective involves selecting suppliers who not only meet quality and cost criteria but also adhere to sustainable practices and contribute positively to society. Like gardeners who choose non-toxic pesticides to protect the ecosystem, procurement managers must consider the broader impact of their choices on the environment and community.

Ethical considerations in procurement management form the bedrock upon which trust, integrity, and fairness are built. Fairness, transparency, accountability, conflict of interest management, and a commitment to sustainability and social responsibility are essential principles that guide ethical procurement practices. By adhering to these principles, organizations can ensure that their procurement activities not only achieve the best outcomes for their projects but also contribute to a more ethical, transparent, and socially responsible business environment.

Project Procurement Management Questions

1. What is the initial phase in the procurement process in project management?
2. How does the selection process in procurement function?

3. What are the key aspects of negotiation in the procurement process?
4. Why is contract management important in procurement?
5. What marks the closure of the procurement process?
6. In procurement planning and execution, what is crucial for identifying procurement needs?
7. How does effective execution of procurements benefit a project?
8. Why is understanding different contract types essential in procurement management?
9. What are the ethical considerations in procurement management?
10. How does a project manager effectively manage contract types and relationships?

Project Procurement Management Answers

1. Answer: The initial phase is thorough planning, which involves identifying the project's needs in terms of materials, equipment, and services, and aligning this with the overall project strategy.

2. Answer: The selection process involves identifying potential suppliers and evaluating them based on criteria like cost, quality, reliability, and service. It includes soliciting and evaluating bids or proposals, then choosing the most suitable supplier.

3. Answer: Negotiation is about finalizing the terms of the contract, focusing not only on price but also on delivery schedules, quality standards, and payment terms. It's a critical step to establish a fair deal for both parties.

4. Answer: Contract management ensures that the supplier adheres to the agreed terms. It involves monitoring the supplier's performance, managing the relationship, and handling issues, ensuring that goods or services meet the specified requirements.

5. Answer: The closure involves evaluating the supplier's performance, making final payments, and documenting lessons learned, which is vital for continuous improvement in future projects.

6. Answer: A thorough analysis of the project scope, schedule, and resources is crucial to accurately identify what needs to be procured, in what quantities, and when.

7. Answer: Effective execution, including issuing RFPs, evaluating bids, negotiating contracts, and managing suppliers, ensures that resources are acquired in a timely, cost-effective, and quality-assured manner, contributing to project success.

8. Answer: Understanding different contract types, such as fixed-price, cost-reimbursable, and time and materials contracts, is essential to choose the right one based on the project's risk profile and requirements.

9. Answer: Ethical considerations include fairness in the supplier selection process, transparency in procurement criteria and decisions, accountability for procurement actions, managing conflicts of interest, and considering sustainability and social responsibility.

10. Answer: This involves negotiating fair terms, managing contracts diligently to ensure compliance, and preparing for and handling risks associated with each contract type.

Chapter 14: Project Examination Content

Comprehensive Overview of the Exam Content

Whether for professional certifications, academic advancement, or any other field, necessitates a deep dive into the essence of the exam content. A comprehensive overview of this content is akin to charting a map for a voyage, outlining the territories to be explored, the challenges to be faced, and the knowledge to be acquired. This overview serves not only as a guide but also as a strategic tool to navigate through the complexities of the examination, ensuring readiness and confidence in the aspirant.

It includes the fundamental theories, concepts, and terminologies that are essential for a nuanced grasp of the topic. Mastery of this foundational knowledge is crucial, as it sets the stage for more advanced exploration and analysis. It's the equivalent of learning the rules of grammar before attempting to write poetry; it's essential for understanding the subtleties and complexities that follow.

Following the foundational knowledge, the exam content typically branches out into specific domains or areas of focus. These domains represent the various facets of the subject matter, each offering a deeper dive into particular themes, processes, and methodologies. For instance, in a project management certification exam, these domains might include project initiation, planning, execution, monitoring and control, and closure. Each domain encompasses a range of topics, detailing the skills, techniques, and best practices relevant to that area. Understanding these domains in depth equips the aspirant with a holistic view of the subject matter, preparing them to tackle scenario-based questions that test their application of knowledge.

A critical component of the exam content is the practical application of knowledge. This aspect evaluates the aspirant's ability to apply theoretical principles to real-world scenarios, solving problems, making decisions, and implementing strategies effectively. It's a testament to the practical relevance of the examination, bridging the gap between academic knowledge and practical skills. Preparation for this component often involves studying case studies, engaging in simulations, or practical exercises that mimic real-life challenges.

Emerging trends and innovations within the field also constitute an important part of the exam content. In a constantly evolving world, staying abreast of the latest developments, technologies, and methodologies is vital. This ensures that the aspirant is not only knowledgeable about the current state of the field but is also forward-thinking, ready to adapt to future changes. This component of the exam content encourages continuous learning and curiosity, traits that are invaluable in any professional or academic pursuit.

Lastly, ethical considerations and professional standards are often integral to the exam content, underscoring the importance of integrity, responsibility, and ethical conduct in the field. This ensures that aspirants not only excel in their technical or theoretical understanding but also in their ethical and professional behavior.

In conclusion, a comprehensive overview of exam content is a multifaceted exploration that includes foundational knowledge, specific domains of focus, practical application, emerging trends, and ethical considerations. This overview is not just a study guide; it's a blueprint for developing a well-rounded, deeply informed understanding of the subject matter, ensuring that aspirants are fully prepared to tackle the examination with confidence and competence.

In-depth Analysis of Exam Topics

An in-depth analysis of exam topics is akin to embarking on a detailed exploration of a vast and diverse landscape. Each topic represents a distinct terrain, rich with its own concepts, theories, and applications. Navigating through these topics requires more than just surface-level understanding; it demands a deep dive into the intricacies of each subject, unraveling the complexities and connecting the dots to form a cohesive understanding.

Foundational topics often encompass the core principles and basic theories that are essential for grasping more complex concepts. Delving into these topics involves not just memorizing facts but understanding the underlying principles that govern the subject matter. It's akin to learning the rules of physics before attempting to understand how a plane flies. Mastery of foundational topics ensures a solid base, enabling learners to tackle more advanced topics with confidence.

Moving beyond the foundations, the analysis progresses to specialized topics. These areas offer a deeper exploration of specific aspects of the subject matter, showcasing the diversity within the field. Specialized topics often require learners to apply foundational knowledge in specific contexts, solving problems, and exploring scenarios that reflect real-world applications. This stage of the analysis is like venturing into different ecosystems within a landscape, each with its unique challenges and characteristics. Engaging with specialized topics not only enhances understanding but also fosters critical thinking and problem-solving skills.

A crucial part of in-depth analysis is the exploration of case studies and practical applications. This involves studying real-life examples to see how theoretical concepts are applied in practice. Case studies bring the subject matter to life, demonstrating its relevance and applicability. This approach allows learners to see the implications of theoretical knowledge in real-world settings, bridging the gap between theory and practice. It's a hands-on experience, like a scientist conducting experiments to observe principles in action. Through case studies, learners gain insights into the practical challenges and solutions within the field, enriching their understanding and preparing them for real-world application.

Emerging trends and recent developments represent another vital area of analysis. In a rapidly evolving world, staying updated with the latest advancements and innovations is crucial. This part of the analysis involves exploring new theories, technologies, methodologies, or changes in professional standards. It's about looking to the horizon, anticipating the future direction of the field. Engaging with emerging trends keeps learners at the cutting edge of the subject matter, fostering a forward-thinking mindset and preparing them for the evolving demands of the field.

Ethical considerations and professional standards are integral to a comprehensive analysis. This aspect examines the moral and ethical implications of the subject matter, emphasizing the importance of ethical conduct, integrity, and professional responsibility. It's a reflection on the impact of one's actions and decisions within the field, underscoring the responsibility that comes with expertise. This analysis ensures that learners not only excel in their technical or theoretical knowledge but also understand the importance of ethical practices and standards in their professional conduct.

An in-depth analysis of exam topics is a comprehensive exploration that covers foundational topics, specialized areas, practical applications, emerging trends, and ethical considerations. It's a holistic approach that prepares learners not just to succeed in exams but to excel in their field, equipped with a deep understanding, practical skills, forward-thinking insights, and a strong ethical foundation. This thorough engagement with the subject matter transforms learners into experts, ready to contribute meaningfully to their field.

Understanding Exam Format, Scoring, and Preparation Techniques

Understanding the exam format, scoring, and preparation techniques is akin to charting a navigational course through unexplored territories. This journey requires not only a map but also an understanding of the terrain and the best strategies for traversing it. Mastery of these aspects ensures that learners can approach their exams with confidence, equipped with the knowledge and skills necessary to achieve success.

The first step in this journey is to understand the exam format. This involves a deep dive into the structure of the exam, including the types of questions (multiple choice, essay, practical tasks), the sections or domains covered, the duration of the exam, and any special instructions or rules. Familiarity with the format is crucial, as it allows learners to tailor their study strategies to the specific demands of the exam. It's similar to understanding the rules of a game before playing it; knowing what to expect enables better preparation and reduces anxiety.

Scoring mechanisms are another critical aspect to understand. This includes knowing how points are allocated for different sections or question types, the passing score, and how incorrect answers are treated (e.g., if there are penalties for wrong answers). Understanding the scoring system allows learners to prioritize their study efforts, focusing on areas that carry the most weight or where they can maximize their score. It's like a mountaineer choosing the best path to ascend a peak, balancing effort with the potential reward.

Preparation techniques are the compass that guides learners through their study journey. Effective preparation starts with setting clear goals and creating a study plan. This plan should outline what topics need to be covered, the timeline for studying, and the methods or resources that will be used. The best study plans are those that are realistic, allowing for flexibility and breaks to prevent burnout. It's about pacing oneself, like a long-distance runner, balancing speed with endurance to reach the finish line.

Active learning strategies are integral to effective exam preparation. This goes beyond passive reading or listening, involving techniques that engage with the material actively. Techniques like self-quizzing, practice exams, flashcards, and teaching concepts to others help reinforce knowledge and aid retention. Active learning is akin to a hands-on workshop, where engagement with the material leads to deeper understanding and long-term memory.

Time management is another essential preparation technique. This involves allocating study time effectively, ensuring that all topics are covered without rushing at the last minute. It also includes managing time during the exam itself, ensuring that there is enough time to answer all questions without feeling rushed. Time management in exam preparation is like a chef timing each component of a meal to perfection, ensuring everything comes together at the right moment.

Dealing with exam anxiety is a crucial part of preparation. Techniques such as mindfulness, deep breathing, and positive visualization can help reduce stress and improve focus. It's important for learners to approach the exam with a calm and positive mindset, viewing it as an opportunity to showcase their knowledge rather than a threat. Managing exam anxiety is like a pilot staying calm under pressure, navigating through turbulence with confidence and skill.

In conclusion, understanding the exam format, scoring, and mastering preparation techniques are critical components of exam success. These elements equip learners with a comprehensive strategy for approaching exams, combining knowledge of the exam structure with effective study methods, time management, and anxiety reduction techniques. Armed with this understanding, learners can navigate the challenges of exam preparation with confidence, ready to achieve their best possible outcome.

Chapter 15: Ethics

Deep Dive into Ethical Responsibilities in Project Management

In the realm of project management, ethical responsibilities are akin to the compass guiding a ship through tumultuous seas. They ensure that decisions and actions not only align with organizational goals but also uphold the highest standards of integrity and respect for all stakeholders involved. A deep dive into ethical responsibilities in project management reveals a complex, multifaceted landscape where every decision can significantly impact the project's outcome and the organization's reputation.

At the core of ethical project management is the commitment to honesty and transparency. This means being truthful about project progress, challenges, and outcomes, even when the news is not positive. It involves presenting accurate information to stakeholders, avoiding the temptation to overpromise or underdeliver. Like a beacon in the dark, honesty illuminates the path forward, fostering trust and credibility among team members, clients, and partners.

Respect for individuals is another critical aspect of ethical project management. This encompasses treating all team members, stakeholders, and suppliers with dignity and consideration, regardless of their role, background, or opinions. It means creating an inclusive environment that values diversity and encourages open dialogue. Respect in project management acts as the foundation for collaborative relationships, ensuring that everyone feels valued and heard.

Confidentiality and the protection of sensitive information are paramount in maintaining ethical integrity. Project managers often have access to proprietary data, personal information, and trade secrets. Safeguarding this information, refraining from disclosing it without authorization, and preventing its misuse are essential duties. Like a guardian of secrets, the project manager must ensure that confidentiality is preserved, protecting the interests of the organization and its stakeholders.

Fairness and impartiality in decision-making are crucial to ethical project management. This involves making choices based on objective criteria rather than personal bias, favoritism, or external pressure. Whether it's selecting suppliers, allocating resources, or resolving conflicts, decisions should be made transparently and equitably. Fairness ensures that the project's best interests are always at the forefront, promoting a culture of integrity and fairness.

Responsibility towards the community and the environment represents a broader dimension of ethical project management. This means considering the social and environmental impact of project activities, striving for sustainability, and contributing positively to the community. Like a steward of the Earth, the project manager must balance project objectives with the responsibility to minimize negative impacts and enhance positive outcomes for society and the environment.

Finally, ethical project management involves a commitment to professional development and continuous improvement. This entails staying updated with industry standards, ethical guidelines, and best practices. It also involves mentoring and guiding team members towards ethical conduct, fostering a culture of learning and accountability.

The ethical responsibilities in project management form the moral fabric that holds the project together, guiding actions and decisions towards the greater good. By adhering to principles of honesty, respect, confidentiality, fairness, social responsibility, and continuous improvement, project managers not only contribute to the success of their projects but also uphold the dignity and integrity of their profession. In doing so, they navigate the complex landscape of project management with a clear ethical compass, ensuring that their journey is not just successful but also honorable.

Exploring PMP's Code of Ethics and Professional Conduct

Integral to this certification is the adherence to a robust Code of Ethics and Professional Conduct, which outlines the moral and professional standards expected of certified professionals. Exploring the PMP's Code of Ethics and Professional Conduct is akin to delving into the philosophical underpinnings of project management, revealing the core values that should guide every decision and action in the field.

Honesty and Integrity

At the heart of the PMP Code of Ethics is the principle of honesty and integrity. This principle demands that project management professionals conduct their work and interactions with transparent honesty, ensuring that all information is communicated truthfully and openly. Integrity compels professionals to stand by their word, fulfill commitments, and own up to their mistakes. It's the ethical cornerstone that builds trust between project managers, their teams, stakeholders, and clients. Like a lighthouse guiding ships safely to shore, honesty and integrity illuminate the path for ethical decision-making and actions in project management.

Respect and Fairness

Respect is another fundamental tenet of the PMP Code of Ethics. It emphasizes the importance of valuing individuals and their contributions, fostering an environment of open communication and mutual respect. This principle extends beyond mere politeness to encompass a genuine appreciation for diverse perspectives, cultures, and opinions. It encourages project managers to listen actively, provide feedback constructively, and engage in dialogue that uplifts and educates.

Closely tied to respect is the principle of fairness, which requires project managers to make decisions impartially and objectively. Fairness involves treating all parties with justice, making equitable decisions free from favoritism or bias. It's about creating equal opportunities for participation and recognition, ensuring that meritocracy prevails in all project-related activities and decisions.

Responsibility and Accountability

The Code also stresses the importance of responsibility and accountability in project management. Professionals are urged to take ownership of their actions and the outcomes of their projects, including any errors or missteps. This principle encourages project managers to make decisions based on the best interests of the project and its stakeholders, considering the broader impacts of their actions on society and the environment. Accountability entails being answerable for the consequences of one's decisions, fostering a culture of transparency and ethical responsibility.

Professionalism and Excellence

Professionalism is a key component of the Code, encapsulating the behaviors and attitudes that define a committed project management professional. This includes adhering to the highest standards of conduct, continuously seeking to improve one's competence, and contributing to the advancement of the project management field. Professionalism demands a commitment to excellence, striving not only to meet but to exceed the expectations set forth by the profession.

Commitment to the Community and the Environment

Finally, the Code highlights the responsibility of project managers to contribute positively to the community and the environment. This involves considering the social and environmental implications of project activities, advocating for sustainable practices, and engaging in activities that benefit society. It's a recognition of the broader role that project management plays in shaping the world, urging professionals to act as stewards of the planet and its people.

Exploring the PMP's Code of Ethics and Professional Conduct reveals a comprehensive framework designed to guide project managers in navigating the ethical complexities of their profession. It serves as a reminder that project management is not just about delivering results but doing so in a manner that upholds the highest ethical standards, respects all stakeholders, and contributes positively to the world. Adherence to this Code ensures that PMP-certified professionals are not only skilled in the technical aspects of project management but also champions of ethical excellence.

Ethical Dilemmas and Decision-Making in Project Management

Navigating the intricate landscape of project management often involves facing ethical dilemmas, where the right course of action is obscured by competing interests, ambiguous circumstances, or the potential for adverse outcomes. These ethical quandaries test the moral compass of project managers, challenging them to make decisions that align with ethical principles while achieving project objectives. Understanding how to approach these dilemmas, and the decision-making processes involved, is crucial for maintaining integrity, trust, and professionalism in project management.

Ethical dilemmas in project management can arise from various situations, such as resource allocation, stakeholder expectations, or conflicts of interest. These dilemmas often present a choice between adhering to ethical standards and pursuing actions that, while potentially beneficial to the project's short-term goals, could compromise ethical integrity. For instance, a project manager might face a dilemma between reporting accurate project delays, potentially jeopardizing stakeholder support, or presenting an overly optimistic timeline to maintain confidence.

Approaching these dilemmas requires a structured decision-making process that begins with identifying the ethical aspects of the situation. This involves discerning the ethical principles at stake, such as honesty, fairness, respect, and responsibility. Like a detective piecing together clues to solve a mystery, the project manager must analyze the situation to understand the ethical dimensions fully.

Once the ethical considerations are identified, the next step involves evaluating the alternatives. This evaluation should consider the consequences of each option, not just in terms of project outcomes but also the impact on stakeholders, the team, and the broader community. It's a process akin to weighing scales, where the project manager must balance the benefits and drawbacks of each choice to determine which aligns best with ethical principles.

Engaging in open dialogue with stakeholders and team members can provide valuable insights during this process. Discussing the dilemma openly can uncover perspectives or solutions that the project manager might not have considered. It fosters a culture of transparency and collective ethical responsibility, ensuring that decisions are made with the broadest possible understanding and support.

In making the final decision, ethical frameworks and professional codes of conduct can serve as guiding lights. These frameworks provide a moral grounding, helping project managers to choose actions that uphold the core values of their profession and organization. Whether it's adhering to the PMI's Code of Ethics and Professional Conduct or applying ethical theories, these resources offer a foundation for making principled decisions.

Implementing the decision with integrity and accountability is the final step in the process. This means taking ownership of the decision, communicating it clearly to all affected parties, and standing ready to address any consequences that arise. It's about leading by example, demonstrating a commitment to ethical standards even in the face of challenges.

Ethical dilemmas and decision-making in project management are about more than finding the right answers; they're about navigating the moral complexities of real-world situations with integrity and wisdom. By approaching these dilemmas with a structured decision-making process, seeking diverse perspectives, and grounding decisions in ethical principles, project managers can navigate the ethical challenges of their profession, maintaining trust, respect, and professional integrity.

Exam Tips

Advanced Preparation Strategies for the Exam

As you approach the zenith of your preparation for an important exam, adopting advanced strategies becomes indispensable. These strategies are not merely about enhancing your study routine but transforming it into a well-oiled machine, capable of propelling you towards excellence. Delving into advanced preparation strategies for the exam is akin to a seasoned navigator charting a course through the most treacherous waters, ensuring safe passage to the desired destination.

Holistic Understanding Over Rote Memorization

The first cornerstone of advanced preparation is prioritizing a holistic understanding of the material over rote memorization. This involves integrating concepts, forming connections between topics, and applying knowledge to real-world scenarios. Like a master chef who knows the science behind each ingredient's reaction, you should delve deep into the "why" and "how" of concepts. Employ techniques such as concept mapping to visually organize and interlink ideas, fostering a deeper, more intuitive understanding of the material.

Active Recall and Spaced Repetition

Leverage the power of active recall and spaced repetition, two scientifically backed methods proven to significantly enhance memory retention. Active recall involves testing yourself on the material without looking at the notes, prompting your brain to retrieve information actively. Combine this with spaced repetition, the practice of reviewing material over increasing intervals of time, to embed knowledge deeply into your long-term memory. Tools like flashcards or apps that utilize these principles can transform your retention rates.

Practice Under Exam Conditions

Simulating exam conditions is an advanced strategy that does more than familiarize you with the exam format. It conditions your mind and body to the unique pressures of the exam environment. Set aside time to complete practice exams within the same time constraints and in a similar setting to the actual exam. This not only bolsters your time management skills but also reduces exam-day anxiety, making the real test feel like yet another practice session.

Interleaved Practice

Interleaved practice, the strategy of mixing different topics or subjects in a single study session, challenges the brain more than studying a single topic at a time. This approach mirrors the unpredictable nature of exam questions and enhances your ability to apply knowledge flexibly. By constantly switching gears, you train your brain to adapt and apply concepts across various scenarios, significantly improving problem-solving skills.

Peer Teaching and Discussion Groups

Engaging in peer teaching sessions or discussion groups is a strategy that benefits all participants. Explaining concepts to peers not only reinforces your own understanding but also highlights areas that need further review.

These sessions can provide new insights into the material, offer alternative problem-solving approaches, and build a support network that keeps motivation high.

Mental and Physical Well-being

Advanced preparation recognizes the integral role of mental and physical well-being in exam performance. Incorporate regular exercise, healthy eating, and sufficient sleep into your preparation routine. Techniques such as meditation or mindfulness can also enhance focus and reduce stress. Like a finely tuned instrument, your body and mind must be in optimal condition to perform at their best.

Advanced preparation strategies for the exam transcend basic study techniques, offering a multifaceted approach that encompasses deep understanding, effective memory techniques, exam simulation, varied practice, collaborative learning, and holistic well-being. By adopting these strategies, you equip yourself not just with knowledge but with the resilience, adaptability, and mental clarity needed to excel in the examination and beyond.

Effective Time Management Techniques for the Exam

Mastering effective time management techniques for an exam is akin to a skilled captain navigating a ship through a maze of islands under a strict time constraint. Each decision on where to steer, how fast to go, and when to pause for assessment significantly impacts the journey's success. For exam takers, the ability to efficiently allocate time across different sections and questions can mean the difference between a rushed, incomplete attempt and a well-executed performance that showcases their knowledge and skills to the fullest.

Understand the Exam Structure

The first step in effective time management is to thoroughly understand the exam's structure. Like a map that outlines the terrain ahead, knowing the format, the number and types of questions, and the allocation of marks provides a strategic overview of where to focus your efforts. This understanding allows you to allocate your time proportionally, ensuring that you spend the right amount of time on each section relative to its weight.

Develop a Time Allocation Plan

Once you're familiar with the exam structure, the next step is to develop a time allocation plan. This involves breaking down the exam duration into segments dedicated to reading instructions, answering questions, reviewing, and, crucially, leaving a buffer for unexpected challenges. Similar to plotting waypoints on a journey, this plan serves as a guide to pace yourself throughout the exam, ensuring that you have enough time to tackle all parts without undue haste.

Practice with Timed Sessions

Implementing timed practice sessions is akin to conducting drills before the main event. By simulating exam conditions and adhering to your time allocation plan, you condition yourself to the rhythm and pace required for the actual exam. This practice helps build speed and efficiency in answering questions, reduces anxiety associated with time pressure, and improves your overall exam performance.

Prioritize Questions

Effective time management also involves strategic decision-making on the spot, particularly when deciding which questions to tackle first. Prioritizing questions based on your strengths, the marks allocated, and the estimated time to answer can optimize your score. It's like choosing the most favorable winds to sail with; answering questions you're confident about first can boost your morale and ensure you secure as many marks as early as possible in the exam.

Monitor Time During the Exam

Constantly monitoring your time during the exam is crucial. Keep a watch or clock in view (if permitted) and periodically check it to ensure you're adhering to your time allocation plan. Adjust as necessary if you find yourself spending too long on a particular question or section. This vigilance is similar to a navigator regularly checking their compass and map to ensure they're on the right path.

Know When to Move On

An essential aspect of time management is knowing when to move on from a question. If you find yourself stuck, it's better to mark it (if the exam format allows) and proceed to the next question rather than getting bogged down. This decision is akin to a captain choosing to circumnavigate an obstacle rather than forcing a direct path through it, preserving resources and momentum for the rest of the journey.

Effective time management techniques for the exam are about more than just watching the clock; they're about strategic planning, practice, prioritization, vigilance, and adaptability. By mastering these techniques, you equip yourself to navigate through the exam efficiently, making the most of the allotted time to showcase your knowledge and skills comprehensively.

Identifying and Avoiding Common Pitfalls

Embarking on any significant endeavor, be it a complex project, a new career path, or an academic pursuit, is fraught with potential pitfalls. These pitfalls, often subtle and insidious, can derail even the most meticulously planned journey. Identifying and avoiding these common pitfalls is akin to a seasoned traveler navigating through treacherous terrain, equipped with the wisdom to recognize dangers and the savvy to avoid them.

Complacency Overconfidence and

One of the most deceptive pitfalls is overconfidence, coupled with complacency. It's the belief that success is guaranteed, leading to a lax attitude towards preparation and vigilance. Like Icarus flying too close to the sun, overconfidence can lead to a dramatic fall. Avoiding this pitfall requires a balance of confidence and humility, recognizing that no matter how skilled or experienced, there is always room for improvement and always a need for thorough preparation.

Failure to Plan Adequately

"Failure to plan is planning to fail," as the adage goes, highlights another common pitfall. Many ventures falter not from a lack of effort or skill but from inadequate planning. This oversight is akin to setting sail without a map; even the strongest winds can't guide you to your destination if you don't know the course. To avoid this pitfall, invest time in meticulous planning, anticipating potential challenges, and devising strategies to navigate them.

Underestimating the Importance of Flexibility

Rigid adherence to a plan, without room for adaptation, is a pitfall that ensnares many. The world is dynamic, filled with unforeseen changes and challenges. A plan that seemed perfect in theory can quickly become obsolete in practice. Avoiding this pitfall requires embracing flexibility, like a reed that bends with the wind but doesn't break. Be prepared to adjust your plans, strategies, and even goals as circumstances evolve.

Neglecting Self-Care

In the pursuit of goals, it's easy to fall into the trap of neglecting self-care. Long hours, high stress, and constant pressure can take a toll on physical and mental health, leading to burnout. This pitfall is akin to neglecting to maintain your vehicle on a long journey; eventually, it will break down. Avoiding this pitfall requires recognizing that self-care is not a luxury but a necessity. Regular rest, healthy habits, and leisure activities are essential for maintaining peak performance over the long term.

Ignoring Feedback and Criticism

Another common pitfall is the refusal to listen to feedback and criticism. While not all criticism is constructive, there is often valuable insight to be gleaned from the perspectives of others. Dismissing feedback out of hand is like navigating with blinders on; you miss the opportunity to see the full picture and make necessary adjustments. To avoid this pitfall, cultivate openness to feedback, learn to sift the constructive from the destructive, and use it as a tool for growth and improvement.

Overlooking the Power of Networking

Finally, underestimating the value of networking and relationships is a pitfall that many encounter. Success is rarely a solo endeavor; it often depends on the support, advice, and opportunities that come from a network of contacts. Neglecting to build and maintain these relationships is like trying to sail a ship without a crew. Avoiding this pitfall involves recognizing the importance of networking, investing time in building relationships, and maintaining them with sincerity and reciprocity.

Identifying and avoiding common pitfalls on the road to success requires a combination of self-awareness, planning, flexibility, self-care, openness to feedback, and an appreciation for the value of relationships. Armed with these strategies, individuals can navigate their paths more smoothly, overcoming obstacles and reaching their destinations with wisdom and grace.

Stress Management and Mental Preparation for the Exam

As the countdown to an important exam begins, the crescendo of stress and anxiety can often seem overwhelming, transforming what should be a showcase of knowledge and skills into a daunting ordeal. However, with the right stress management techniques and mental preparation, this tide can be turned, allowing examinees to approach their exams with calmness and confidence.

Embracing a Positive Mindset

The foundation of effective exam preparation lies in cultivating a positive mindset. It's about shifting from a perspective of fear and apprehension to one of opportunity and challenge. Visualize success rather than dwelling on the possibility of failure. Imagine walking out of the exam room, feeling satisfied with your performance. This mental rehearsal not only boosts confidence but also reduces anxiety, setting a positive tone for your preparation and performance.

Structured Study Plan

A well-structured study plan is your roadmap through the maze of exam preparation. It breaks down the overwhelming task into manageable chunks, ensuring comprehensive coverage of the material without the panic of last-minute cramming. Allocate specific times for study, breaks, and revisions, making sure to balance your workload to avoid burnout. The certainty of a plan provides a sense of control, significantly lowering stress levels.

Relaxation Techniques

Incorporating relaxation techniques into your daily routine can be a game-changer for managing stress. Practices such as deep breathing exercises, meditation, or yoga not only calm the mind but also improve concentration and memory retention. Even short breaks spent practicing these techniques can recharge your batteries and reduce the physiological symptoms of stress, preparing you mentally and physically for the exam ahead.

Healthy Lifestyle Choices

Never underestimate the power of physical health on mental performance. A balanced diet, regular exercise, and adequate sleep are the pillars supporting your exam preparation. Exercise, in particular, is an excellent stress reliever, releasing endorphins that act as natural mood lifters. Meanwhile, a good night's sleep consolidates learning and memory, ensuring you're mentally sharp on exam day.

Support System

Lean on your support system during this time. Discussing your anxieties with friends, family, or fellow students can provide emotional relief and sometimes offer new insights or strategies for your preparation. Knowing you're not alone in your exam journey can alleviate feelings of isolation and stress.

Managing stress and mentally preparing for an exam is a multifaceted approach that encompasses maintaining a positive mindset, following a structured study plan, utilizing relaxation techniques, making healthy lifestyle choices, and seeking support. By adopting these strategies, you can transform exam stress into a motivating force, propelling you towards achieving your best performance.

Last-minute Study Tips and Tricks

As the clock ticks down to exam day, the pressure mounts, and the need for effective last-minute study strategies becomes paramount. This period, often fraught with anxiety and stress, demands a focused approach to maximize retention and readiness. Here are some distilled tips and tricks for those crucial final hours, designed to sharpen your recall and boost your confidence as you step into the exam room.

Prioritize and Condense

Begin by prioritizing the topics based on their weight in the exam and your level of comfort with each. Concentrate on areas that offer the highest return on investment. Creating condensed notes or cheat sheets for these areas can be incredibly effective. Summarize key concepts, formulas, and definitions in a compact format, focusing on the essence of the topics. This process not only aids in last-minute revision but also enhances memory retention by rephrasing and summarizing the content.

Active Recall and Testing

Leverage the power of active recall and self-testing, which are among the most efficient ways to enhance memory. Instead of passively rereading your notes, test yourself on the material. Use flashcards, practice questions, or even try to recite information from memory. This technique forces your brain to retrieve information actively, strengthening memory pathways and aiding in quicker recall during the exam.

Teach What You've Learned

Explaining the material to someone else is a powerful tool for understanding and retention. Teaching forces you to organize your knowledge, clarify your thoughts, and identify any gaps in your understanding. If you can't find a study buddy, pretend you're teaching the material to an imaginary audience, or even talk aloud to yourself. This process can solidify your grasp on the material and reveal areas that might need a quick review.

Utilize Mnemonics

Mnemonics are shortcuts that help you remember complex information through patterns, acronyms, or vivid stories. Creating memorable and sometimes humorous associations with the material can make it easier to recall facts, sequences, or lists during the exam. This technique is particularly useful for subjects that involve memorization of terminology, processes, or sequences.

Practice Under Exam Conditions

Simulate exam conditions by timing yourself while answering practice questions or taking a practice test. This not only familiarizes you with the timing pressure but also helps in managing exam-day anxiety. Understanding how to allocate your time effectively across questions can be a critical advantage when you're in the actual exam.

Rest and Relax

While it might seem counterintuitive when time is of the essence, ensuring you get enough rest before the exam is crucial. A well-rested mind is more alert, focused, and capable of critical thinking and recall. Incorporate short breaks during your study sessions to avoid burnout, and try relaxation techniques such as deep breathing or meditation to calm pre-exam nerves.

Visualize Success

Spend a few minutes visualizing a successful exam experience. Picture yourself calmly answering the questions, recalling information smoothly, and leaving the exam room satisfied with your performance. Positive visualization can reduce anxiety and boost your confidence, setting a positive tone for the exam day.

In conclusion, effective last-minute study isn't about cramming as much information as possible; it's about strategic review, prioritization, and mental preparation. By focusing on high-yield topics, actively engaging with the material, and maintaining a positive, calm mindset, you can maximize your performance even in the final hours before the exam. Remember, the goal is not just to pass the exam but to do so with confidence and clarity.

Mock Exam

1. What is the primary objective of the 'Identify Stakeholders' process?

- A) To list the project tasks and assign them to team members.

- B) To determine who may affect or be affected by the project and analyze their expectations.

- C) To establish the project's scope statement.

- D) To allocate the budget among stakeholders based on their influence.

- Correct Answer: B

2. Why is 'Plan Scope Management' crucial in project management?

- A) It outlines how the project scope will be defined, validated, and controlled.

- B) It directly assigns tasks to project team members.

- C) It establishes the project schedule and milestones.

- D) It allocates financial resources to scope-related activities.

- Correct Answer: A

3. The 'Define Scope' process is important because it:

- A) Determines the cost of project activities.

- B) Develops a detailed description of the project and product.

- C) Assigns resources to project tasks.

- D) Lists all the stakeholders involved in the project.

- Correct Answer: B

4. 'Create WBS' (Work Breakdown Structure) is essential for:

- A) Allocating the project budget.

- B) Breaking down project deliverables into smaller, more manageable components.

- C) Defining the project's critical path.

- D) Assigning tasks to the project team.

- Correct Answer: B

5. In 'Project Schedule Management', the main purpose of 'Sequence Activities' is to:

- A) Allocate the project's budget across its activities.

- B) Identify and document relationships between project activities.

- C) Estimate the duration of each project activity.

- D) Assign project team members to specific tasks.

- Correct Answer: B

6. 'Estimate Activity Durations' is a critical process because it:

- A) Defines the specific actions needed to complete project work.

- B) Determines the number of work periods needed to complete individual activities.

- C) Allocates resources to project activities.

- D) Develops the project budget.

- Correct Answer: B

7. The 'Develop Schedule' process aims to:

- A) Identify the project's critical path.

- B) Allocate additional resources to project activities.

- C) Aggregate the estimated durations of all activities to establish the project timeline.

- D) Assign specific start and end dates to project activities.

- Correct Answer: C

8. 'Control Schedule' ensures that:

- A) The schedule management plan is strictly followed without any changes.

- B) Any changes to the project schedule are recorded and assessed for impact on the project timeline.

- C) Project activities are completed as quickly as possible, regardless of quality.

- D) Resources are over-allocated to guarantee project completion.

- Correct Answer: B

9. The primary goal of 'Plan Cost Management' is to:

- A) Estimate the costs associated with each project activity.

- B) Set the policies, procedures, and documentation for planning, managing, expending, and controlling project costs.

- C) Allocate the project budget across tasks.

- D) Finalize the project budget.

- Correct Answer: B

10. Why is the 'Estimate Costs' process critical?

- A) It approves the project budget.

- B) It identifies the amount of money needed to complete project activities.

- C) It allocates the budget across project phases.

- D) It reduces project costs.

- Correct Answer: B

11. The 'Determine Budget' process is vital because it:

- A) Allocates resources to project activities.

- B) Aggregates the estimated costs of individual activities or work packages to establish an authorized cost baseline.

- C) Identifies potential financial risks to the project.

- D) Cuts the project's overall costs.

- Correct Answer: B

12. In 'Control Costs', a primary function is to:

- A) Continuously increase the project budget to meet changing needs.

- B) Monitor the status of the project to update the cost forecast and manage changes to the cost baseline.

- C) Assign the project budget to specific team members.

- D) Estimate the costs of project activities.

- Correct Answer: B

13. 'Plan Quality Management' is designed to:

- A) Perform quality control tests on project deliverables.

- B) Identify quality requirements and/or standards for the project and its deliverables, and document how the project will demonstrate compliance.

- C) Implement the quality management plan.

- D) Reduce the costs associated with ensuring quality.

- Correct Answer: B

14. The 'Manage Quality' process focuses on:

- A) Reducing the number of quality audits required.

- B) Translating the quality management plan into executable quality activities that incorporate the organization's quality policies.

- C) Correcting defects in project deliverables.

- D) Allocating resources for quality management activities.

- Correct Answer: B

15. Why is 'Control Quality' important in project management?

- A) It ensures that the project adheres to its budget.

- B) It verifies that project deliverables meet the required standards and stakeholder expectations.

- C) It develops the project management plan.

- D) It enhances stakeholder engagement.

- Correct Answer: B

16. 'Identify Risks' process is fundamental because it:

- A) Directly leads to the development of the project risk management plan.

- B) Helps to ensure that potential project risks are identified, documented, and analyzed.

- C) Allocates the project budget to cover identified risks.

- D) Implements immediate risk responses.

- Correct Answer: B

17. 'Perform Qualitative Risk Analysis' is crucial for:

- A) Assigning a numerical value to the impact of risks.

- B) Prioritizing risks based on their likelihood and potential impact on project objectives.

- C) Identifying new risks throughout the project lifecycle.

- D) Allocating budget to mitigate identified risks.

- Correct Answer: B

18. The goal of 'Perform Quantitative Risk Analysis' is to:

- A) Develop options to enhance opportunities and reduce threats.

- B) Numerically assess the effect of identified risks on overall project objectives.

- C) Assign qualitative ratings to risks based on their severity.

- D) Implement risk responses for high-priority risks.

- Correct Answer: B

19. 'Plan Risk Responses' is essential for:

- A) Developing strategies to minimize potential threats and maximize opportunities.

- B) Identifying project risks.

- C) Quantifying the financial impact of risks on the project.

- D) Monitoring residual risks.

- Correct Answer: A

20. 'Implement Risk Responses' ensures that:

- A) Risk management efforts are proactive rather than reactive.

114

- B) Risk response plans are executed and their effectiveness is evaluated.

- C) All project risks are eliminated.

- D) The project budget includes a contingency for risks.

- Correct Answer: B

21. The purpose of 'Monitor Risks' is to:

- A) Prevent any new risks from occurring.

- B) Track identified risks, monitor residual risks, and identify new risks, ensuring effective risk management throughout the project.

- C) Allocate additional budget for unforeseen risks.

- D) Update the risk management plan periodically.

- Correct Answer: B

22. 'Plan Procurement Management' results in the creation of:

- A) Purchase orders for project resources.

- B) A procurement management plan that outlines how procurement processes will be conducted.

- C) Finalized contracts with selected vendors.

- D) A detailed list of potential sellers.

- Correct Answer: B

23. The 'Conduct Procurements' process is primarily concerned with:

- A) Estimating the costs associated with procurements.

- B) Obtaining seller responses, selecting sellers, and awarding contracts.

- C) Developing a procurement strategy for the project.

- D) Closing procurements and finalizing contracts.

- Correct Answer: B

24. Why is 'Manage Stakeholder Engagement' crucial?

- A) It ensures stakeholders are only informed about project decisions after they're made.

- B) It involves seeking stakeholder input and addressing their concerns to ensure their continued engagement.

- C) It identifies stakeholders' communication preferences.

- D) It documents stakeholders' influence on the project.

- Correct Answer: B

25. The 'Monitor Stakeholder Engagement' process is key for:

- A) Identifying new stakeholders not previously engaged.

- B) Adjusting strategies and plans for stakeholder engagement based on ongoing monitoring and feedback.

- C) Documenting resolved stakeholder issues for future reference.

- D) Reducing the influence of stakeholders on the project.

- Correct Answer: B

26. 'Define Activities' process in project management is crucial because it:

- A) Identifies the specific actions to be performed to produce project deliverables.

- B) Assigns project resources to specific tasks.

- C) Estimates the cost of project activities.

- D) Develops the project schedule.

- Correct Answer: A

27. The main objective of 'Sequence Activities' is to:

- A) Allocate resources to project activities.

- B) Identify dependencies between activities.

- C) Estimate the duration of project activities.

- D) Develop the project budget.

- Correct Answer: B

28. Why is 'Estimate Activity Resources' important?

- A) It defines the project scope.

- B) It determines the type and quantities of resources required for each activity.

- C) It assigns responsibilities to team members.

- D) It creates the project schedule.

- Correct Answer: B

29. In 'Develop Schedule', a critical output is:

- A) The project budget.

- B) The project charter.

- C) The schedule baseline.

- D) The stakeholder register.

- Correct Answer: C

30. 'Control Schedule' process ensures that:

- A) The project schedule is not changed.

- B) The project is completed as per the approved schedule baseline.

- C) All project activities are completed on time.

- D) Additional resources are allocated to speed up the project.

- Correct Answer: B

31. 'Plan Cost Management' establishes:

- A) The project's cost baseline.

- B) Guidelines for how costs will be managed and controlled.

- C) The total project budget.

- D) Specific costs for project activities.

- Correct Answer: B

32. The 'Estimate Costs' process is critical for providing:

- A) A detailed project schedule.

- B) An assessment of the probable costs of project work.

- C) The project's quality metrics.

- D) A list of project risks.

- Correct Answer: B

33. 'Determine Budget' process is important because it:

- A) Identifies all possible project expenses.

- B) Aggregates the estimated costs of individual activities to establish an authorized cost baseline.

- C) Allocates additional funds for project risks.

- D) Reduces the overall project costs.

- Correct Answer: B

34. In 'Control Costs', a key activity is:

- A) Approving project changes.

- B) Monitoring project expenditure against the cost baseline.

- C) Allocating the project budget.

- D) Reducing project costs.

- Correct Answer: B

35. The 'Plan Quality Management' process aims to:

- A) Inspect project deliverables for defects.

- B) Ensure the project will satisfy the needs for which it was undertaken.

- C) Implement the quality management plan.

- D) Reduce the amount of quality audits.

- Correct Answer: B

36. 'Manage Quality' differs from 'Control Quality' in that it:

- A) Focuses on adherence to quality standards while the project deliverables are being developed.

- B) Is concerned with the overall management of the project's quality policies.

- C) Deals exclusively with the inspection of project outcomes.

- D) Aims to reduce the cost of quality.

- Correct Answer: B

37. The 'Control Quality' process is vital for:

- A) Documenting project progress.

- B) Verifying that project deliverables meet the agreed-upon quality standards.

- C) Developing the project management plan.

- D) Enhancing stakeholder engagement.

- Correct Answer: B

38. 'Identify Risks' process is fundamental because it:

- A) Quantifies the impact of risks on project objectives.

- B) Ensures all potential project risks are identified and documented.

- C) Directly leads to the creation of the risk management plan.

- D) Assigns risk owners to manage specific risks.

- Correct Answer: B

39. 'Perform Qualitative Risk Analysis' process is essential for:

- A) Calculating the numerical probability of risk occurrence.

- B) Prioritizing risks based on their impact and likelihood.

- C) Identifying new risks throughout the project lifecycle.

- D) Allocating the budget to mitigate identified risks.

- Correct Answer: B

40. In 'Perform Quantitative Risk Analysis', the primary goal is to:

- A) Develop strategies to enhance opportunities.

- B) Numerically analyze the effect of identified risks on project objectives.

- C) Assign qualitative ratings to project risks.

- D) Implement immediate risk responses.

- Correct Answer: B

41. 'Plan Risk Responses' focuses on:

- A) Identifying project risks.

- B) Developing options to enhance opportunities and reduce threats.

- C) Monitoring residual risks.

- D) Quantifying the probability and impact of risks.

- Correct Answer: B

42. 'Implement Risk Responses' is important for:

- A) Immediately addressing all identified project risks.

- B) Carrying out agreed-upon risk response strategies.

- C) Continuously identifying new risks.

- D) Quantifying the impact of risks on the project budget.

- Correct Answer: B

43. The main purpose of 'Monitor Risks' is to:

- A) Eliminate all project risks.

- B) Keep track of identified risks, monitor residual risks, and identify new risks, ensuring that risk response plans are effective.

- C) Allocate additional funds to cover potential risks.

- D) Update the risk management plan.

- Correct Answer: B

44. 'Plan Procurement Management' process results in:

- A) Finalization of purchase orders.

- B) Documentation of project purchasing decisions and identification of potential sellers.

- C) Closure of procurement contracts.

- D) Selection of project vendors.

- Correct Answer: B

45. 'Conduct Procurements' primarily involves:

- A) Budgeting for procurement activities.

- B) Receiving seller responses and selecting sellers.

- C) Developing the procurement management plan.

- D) Managing procurement relationships.

- Correct Answer: B

46. Why is 'Manage Stakeholder Engagement' crucial?

- A) It ensures that stakeholders are aware of project decisions after they have been made.

- B) It actively involves stakeholders in the decision-making process, addressing their concerns as they arise.

- C) It identifies stakeholders' communication preferences.

- D) It documents stakeholders' influence on the project.

- Correct Answer: B

47. The 'Monitor Stakeholder Engagement' process is key for:

- A) Initially identifying project stakeholders.

- B) Ensuring stakeholders' needs and expectations are met by adjusting engagement strategies and plans.

- C) Documenting the history of stakeholder interactions.

- D) Reducing the influence of negative stakeholders.

- Correct Answer: B

48. 'Control Resources' process is important to:

- A) Ensure that project resources are allocated according to the plan.

- B) Increase the efficiency of resource utilization.

- C) Prevent any changes to the resource management plan.

- D) Manage the physical resources only, not the team.

- Correct Answer: A

49. In 'Plan Resource Management', the main objective is to:

- A) Assign project tasks to available resources.

- B) Detail how project resources will be identified, acquired, managed, and released.

- C) Develop a schedule for resource utilization.

- D) Estimate the costs associated with project resources.

- Correct Answer: B

50. 'Estimate Activity Resources' process aims to:

- A) Define the types and quantities of resources required for each project activity.

- B) Allocate the project budget across resources.

- C) Develop a comprehensive list of project activities.

- D) Assign specific team members to project tasks.

- Correct Answer: A

51. The 'Manage Project Knowledge' process is designed to:

- A) Document the project's lessons learned and knowledge gained for future use.

- B) Ensure that the project team has access to required informational resources throughout the project.

- C) Facilitate the creation of the project's knowledge management system.

- D) Monitor and control the distribution of project knowledge.

- Correct Answer: A

52. In 'Project Schedule Management', the 'Critical Path Method' (CPM) is used to:

- A) Estimate the shortest project duration and identify which activities have zero float.

- B) Allocate additional resources to non-critical activities to ensure timely project completion.

- C) Identify dependencies between project tasks.

- D) Reduce the project schedule by overlapping activities.

- Correct Answer: A

53. 'Cost-Benefit Analysis' in the 'Plan Risk Responses' process is important for:

- A) Identifying the most cost-effective way to mitigate risks.

- B) Determining the project's budget based on identified risks.

- C) Allocating the correct amount of resources to each identified risk.

- D) Understanding the potential return on investment for risk response actions.

- Correct Answer: D

54. The primary purpose of 'Develop Project Charter' is to:

- A) Outline the project's detailed scope, budget, and schedule.

- B) Formally authorize the existence of a project and provide the project manager with the authority to apply organizational resources.

- C) Assign project team members and define their roles and responsibilities.

- D) Establish communication guidelines for stakeholders.

- Correct Answer: B

55. 'Stakeholder Engagement Assessment Matrix' is used in which process to analyze current versus desired stakeholder engagement levels?

- A) Identify Stakeholders

- B) Plan Stakeholder Engagement

- C) Manage Stakeholder Engagement

- D) Monitor Stakeholder Engagement

- Correct Answer: D

56. In 'Project Scope Management', the process of 'Control Scope' is critical for ensuring that:

- A) The project includes all the work required, and only the work required, to complete the project successfully.

- B) Any changes to the project scope are reflected in the scope baseline.

- C) The project scope is accurately communicated to all stakeholders.

- D) Scope creep is encouraged to accommodate evolving stakeholder requirements.

- Correct Answer: A

57. 'Resource Leveling' is a technique used to:

- A) Extend the project duration due to constraints on resource availability.

- B) Increase the project budget to hire additional resources.

- C) Decrease the amount of resources required for the project.

- D) Ensure resources are worked at their maximum capacity.

- Correct Answer: A

58. The 'Plan Communications Management' process results in:

- A) A detailed project schedule.

- B) An updated risk management plan.

- C) A communications management plan that outlines how project communications will be planned, structured, and monitored.

- D) A stakeholder engagement plan.

- Correct Answer: C

59. 'Qualitative Risk Analysis' must be performed:

- A) Only at the beginning of the project.

- B) Throughout the project lifecycle as new risks can be identified at any stage.

- C) Immediately before the project closure to ensure all risks have been managed.

- D) Once during the planning phase and not repeated.

- Correct Answer: B

60. In 'Project Quality Management', 'Quality Audits' differ from 'Quality Control Measurements' in that audits:

- A) Focus exclusively on the cost implications of meeting quality standards.

- B) Are designed to identify ways to eliminate causes of unsatisfactory performance and quality.

- C) Directly inspect and measure the quality of project deliverables.

- D) Are conducted by external auditors only.

- Correct Answer: B

61. The 'Identify Risks' process is vital because it:

- A) Allows for the quantitative analysis of all identified risks.

- B) Helps to ensure that the project plan is comprehensive and includes contingencies for unknowns.

- C) Provides a mechanism for allocating the project budget to cover identified risks.

- D) Facilitates the immediate implementation of risk responses.

- Correct Answer: B

62. In the 'Monitor and Control Project Work' process, a major activity is to:

- A) Directly manage the execution of the project work.

- B) Review and analyze the performance of the project to meet management objectives.

- C) Update the project management plan and project documents.

- D) Develop detailed descriptions of the project and product.

- Correct Answer: B

63. 'Earned Value Management' (EVM) integrates which three project management values?

- A) Planned Value (PV), Actual Cost (AC), and Earned Value (EV).

- B) Actual Duration (AD), Estimated Cost (EC), and Actual Work (AW).

- C) Cost Variance (CV), Schedule Variance (SV), and Resource Allocation (RA).

- D) Work Performance Data (WPD), Work Performance Information (WPI), and Work Performance Reports (WPR).

- Correct Answer: A

64. The 'Develop Project Team' process is essential because:

- A) It assigns project tasks to the project team members.

- B) It enhances team members' skills, interaction, and overall team environment to improve project performance.

- C) It develops the project management plan.

- D) It ensures that the project team adheres to the budget.

- Correct Answer: B

65. What is the goal of 'Plan Stakeholder Engagement'?

- A) To list all potential stakeholders and their information.

- B) To document how to engage stakeholders and manage their expectations and impact on the project.

- C) To assign project roles and responsibilities to stakeholders.

- D) To approve or reject stakeholder requests.

- Correct Answer: B

66. 'Analogous Estimating' is particularly useful when:

- A) Precise project details are available.

- B) The project is similar to past projects, and historical data is used for estimation.

- C) A detailed and accurate estimate is not required.

- D) The project team demands the highest estimation accuracy.

- Correct Answer: B

67. The 'Perform Integrated Change Control' process ensures that:

- A) All requested changes are automatically approved to avoid delays.

- B) Every change request is thoroughly reviewed, evaluated, and approved, deferred, or rejected.

- C) Changes to the project scope are implemented without formal review and approval.

- D) The project team can bypass the change control process in urgent situations.

- Correct Answer: B

68. 'Plan Communications Management' is designed to:

- A) Restrict the flow of project information.

- B) Define, document, and manage the sending, receiving, and understanding of project information.

- C) Ensure the project team communicates only through formal channels.

- D) Develop the project's organizational chart.

- Correct Answer: B

69. Performing 'Quantitative Risk Analysis' is crucial for projects that:

- A) Are small in scale and complexity.

- B) Require detailed analysis of the potential impact of risks on project objectives.

- C) Do not have any identified risks.

- D) Need to allocate all their budget towards risk mitigation.

- Correct Answer: B

70. 'Control Costs' involves:

- A) Defining the project's budget baseline.

- B) Monitoring project status to update the cost forecasts and manage changes to the cost baseline.

- C) Approving project expenditures as they occur.

- D) Cutting project costs to improve profitability.

- Correct Answer: B

71. Why is 'Monitor and Control Project Work' important?

- A) It ensures that project work is executed according to the project management plan.

- B) It involves tracking, reviewing, and regulating the progress to meet the performance objectives defined in the project management plan.

- C) It is focused solely on controlling the project team's performance.

- D) It manages the project's budget and financial expenditures.

- Correct Answer: B

72. 'Earned Value Management' (EVM) is an effective tool for tracking:

- A) The physical performance of the project against the project plan.

- B) The project's performance in terms of scope, time, and cost.

- C) Only the cost performance of the project.

- D) The quality of project deliverables.

- Correct Answer: B

73. The 'Develop Project Team' process aims to:

- A) Define the project roles and responsibilities.

- B) Enhance the ability of team members to function effectively.

- C) Assign project tasks to team members.

- D) Establish the project's organizational structure.

- Correct Answer: B

74. 'Plan Stakeholder Engagement' results in the creation of:

- A) A stakeholder register.

- B) A stakeholder engagement plan that outlines strategies for engaging stakeholders throughout the project lifecycle.

- C) A risk management plan that addresses stakeholder-related risks.

- D) A communication plan that specifies how stakeholders will be informed.

- Correct Answer: B

75. The purpose of 'Analogous Estimating' is to:

- A) Provide a detailed and accurate estimate based on the assessment of individual project components.

- B) Estimate project duration or cost by comparing the project to similar ones in the past.

- C) Use statistical methods to predict project costs.

- D) Break down the project into smaller parts for more accurate estimation.

- Correct Answer: B

76. What is the primary purpose of 'Develop Project Management Plan' process?

- A) To document the actions necessary to define, prepare, integrate, and coordinate all subsidiary plans.

- B) To establish the project's scope, schedule, and cost baselines.

- C) To assign project tasks to team members.

- D) To approve the project budget and schedule.

- Correct Answer: A

77. In the 'Plan Schedule Management' process, what is the main objective?

- A) To identify the project's critical path.

- B) To establish the policies, procedures, and documentation for planning, developing, managing, executing, and controlling the project schedule.

- C) To allocate resources to project tasks.

- D) To define project activities.

- Correct Answer: B

78. Why is 'Collect Requirements' crucial for project success?

- A) It ensures that the project budget is sufficient.

- B) It defines the project scope based on stakeholder needs and expectations.

- C) It sets the schedule for project delivery.

- D) It allocates project resources efficiently.

- Correct Answer: B

79. 'Define Scope' process in project management primarily involves:

- A) Breaking down project deliverables into smaller components.

- B) Developing a detailed description of the project and product.

- C) Identifying the project's high-level deliverables.

- D) Assigning tasks to project team members.

- Correct Answer: B

80. What is the significance of 'Create WBS' in project management?

- A) It outlines the project's communication plan.

- B) It provides a step-by-step procedure for project delivery.

- C) It breaks down project deliverables into smaller, more manageable components.

- D) It assigns responsibilities to project team members.

- Correct Answer: C

81. In 'Project Schedule Management', what is the primary goal of 'Define Activities'?

- A) To identify specific actions to be performed to produce project deliverables.

- B) To assign project team members to tasks.

- C) To establish the project's milestones.

- D) To allocate the budget across project tasks.

- Correct Answer: A

82. 'Sequence Activities' process in project management is essential for:

- A) Allocating resources to project activities.

- B) Identifying and documenting relationships among project activities.

- C) Establishing the project budget.

- D) Defining the scope of the project.

- Correct Answer: B

83. What is the outcome of 'Estimate Activity Durations'?

- A) A detailed project schedule.

- B) An approximation of the time each activity will take to complete.

- C) The total project duration.

- D) Resource allocation plan for project activities.

- Correct Answer: B

84. 'Develop Schedule' process in project management aims to:

- A) Assign tasks to team members.

- B) Establish the project's milestones and deadlines.

- C) Produce a schedule model that demonstrates how project objectives will be achieved.

- D) Allocate the project budget.

- Correct Answer: C

85. The 'Control Schedule' process is crucial for ensuring:

- A) The project is executed as per the schedule baseline.

- B) Changes to the project schedule are approved.

- C) The project team adheres to the approved schedule.

- D) Project activities are performed on time.

- Correct Answer: A

86. What is the main focus of 'Plan Cost Management'?

- A) To estimate the costs of project activities.

- B) To establish the procedures, policies, and documentation for planning, managing, expending, and controlling project costs.

- C) To allocate the project budget across tasks.

- D) To approve the project budget.

- Correct Answer: B

87. Why is 'Estimate Costs' important in project management?

- A) It approves the project budget.

- B) It provides a basis for determining the project's cost performance.

- C) It approximates the monetary resources needed for project activities.

- D) It allocates the budget to project phases.

- Correct Answer: C

88. The primary purpose of 'Determine Budget' is to:

- A) Allocate resources efficiently.

- B) Aggregate the estimated costs of individual activities or work packages to establish an authorized cost baseline.

- C) Approve additional funds for the project.

- D) Reduce project costs.

- Correct Answer: B

89. What is the significance of 'Control Costs' in project management?

- A) To ensure project expenses do not exceed the authorized funding.

- B) To allocate additional funds to project activities.

- C) To reduce the overall project budget.

- D) To establish the project's cost baseline.

- Correct Answer: A

90. In 'Project Quality Management', the 'Plan Quality Management' process aims to:

- A) Inspect project deliverables for defects.

- B) Identify quality requirements and standards for the project and its deliverables.

- C) Implement the project's quality improvement plan.

- D) Allocate budget for quality control activities.

- Correct Answer: B

91. The 'Manage Quality' process is designed to:

- A) Reduce the cost of quality.

- B) Translate the quality management plan into executable quality practices that incorporate the organization's quality policies.

- C) Correct defects in project deliverables.

- D) Allocate resources for quality management activities.

- Correct Answer: B

92. Why is 'Control Quality' critical in project management?

- A) It ensures the project adheres to the budget.

- B) It focuses on continuous process improvement.

- C) It verifies that project deliverables meet the required quality standards.

- D) It develops the project's Quality Management Plan.

- Correct Answer: C

93. The 'Identify Risks' process in project management is important because it:

- A) Quantifies the impact of risks on project objectives.

- B) Helps in the prioritization of risks for further analysis or action.

- C) Ensures that the project is completed on time and within budget.

- D) Establishes the project's risk management policies and procedures.

- Correct Answer: B

94. In the 'Perform Qualitative Risk Analysis' process, risks are:

- A) Quantified in terms of probability and impact on project objectives.

129

- B) Prioritized based on their probability of occurrence and potential impact.

- C) Mitigated through the development of risk response plans.

- D) Identified and documented for further analysis.

- Correct Answer: B

95. The 'Perform Quantitative Risk Analysis' process is conducted to:

- A) Develop risk response strategies for high-priority risks.

- B) Numerically analyze the effect of identified risks on overall project objectives.

- C) Assign qualitative labels to risks based on their severity.

- D) Determine the project's risk tolerance levels.

- Correct Answer: B

96. 'Plan Risk Responses' is essential for:

- A) Identifying new risks throughout the project lifecycle.

- B) Developing options and actions to enhance opportunities and reduce threats to project objectives.

- C) Quantifying the probability and impact of risks on the project.

- D) Monitoring identified risks and identifying new risks.

- Correct Answer: B

97. hy is the 'Implement Risk Responses' process important?

- A) It ensures risks are identified early in the project.

- B) It applies risk response plans and tracks identified risks, evaluating their effectiveness.

- C) It quantifies the financial impact of risks on the project.

- D) It identifies new risks for the project.

- Correct Answer: B

98. The 'Monitor Risks' process aims to:

- A) Eliminate all risks from the project.

- B) Track identified risks, monitor residual risks, and identify new risks, ensuring risk responses are effective.

- C) Develop new risk response strategies for all identified risks.

- D) Allocate additional budget to cover potential risks identified in the risk register.

- Correct Answer: B

99. In 'Project Procurement Management', the 'Plan Procurement Management' process:

- A) Executes the purchase or acquisition of products, services, or results needed from outside the project team.

- B) Documents project purchasing decisions, specifies the approach, and identifies potential sellers.

- C) Involves the agreement closure process for completed contracts.

- D) Assigns procurement officers to manage vendor contracts.

- Correct Answer: B

100. **The 'Conduct Procurements' process in project management is primarily concerned with:**

- A) Developing the procurement management plan.

- B) Obtaining seller responses, selecting a seller, and awarding a contract.

- C) Closing procurements upon project completion.

- D) Reviewing and approving invoices from vendors and suppliers.

- Correct Answer: B

101. **'Stakeholder Analysis' in the 'Identify Stakeholders' process is crucial for:**

- A) Documenting the impact of stakeholders on the project.

- B) Understanding stakeholders' needs, expectations, and potential impact on the project.

- C) Assigning project tasks to stakeholders based on their influence.

- D) Estimating the budget required for stakeholder management activities.

- Correct Answer: B

102. **In 'Project Scope Management', the main purpose of 'Validate Scope' is to:**

- A) Incorporate changes into the project scope.

- B) Ensure the project's deliverables are completed satisfactorily.

- C) Break down the project scope into smaller, manageable parts.

- D) Define and document the project and product objectives.

- Correct Answer: B

103. **'Critical Chain Method' in project schedule management is used to:**

- A) Identify the longest sequence of dependent tasks that drive the project's duration.

- B) Add buffers to protect the project's delivery date.

- C) Allocate resources across all project activities evenly.

- D) Calculate the total float for project activities.

- Correct Answer: B

104. **The 'Perform Integrated Change Control' process is key for ensuring:**

- A) All proposed changes are implemented immediately to avoid delays.

- B) Changes are reviewed, approved, or rejected by the project's Change Control Board (CCB).

- C) The project plan remains unchanged throughout the project lifecycle.

- D) Stakeholders have direct control over project changes without formal review.

- Correct Answer: B

105. **In 'Project Cost Management', 'Earned Value Analysis' (EVA) is primarily used to:**

- A) Estimate the project's initial budget.

- B) Track the project's performance in terms of scope, time, and cost.

- C) Allocate additional funds to project activities.

- D) Reduce the overall project costs by identifying non-essential activities.

- Correct Answer: B

106. **The 'Develop Project Charter' process is important because it:**

- A) Details the project's deliverables and milestones.

- B) Provides formal authorization for the project to begin.

- C) Assigns specific tasks to project team members.

- D) Establishes the project's final budget.

- Correct Answer: B

107. **'Resource Leveling' is a technique used in project schedule management to:**

- A) Decrease the resources required for project completion.

- B) Address the over-allocation of resources without changing the project scope.

- C) Increase project duration by adding more tasks.

- D) Assign the most skilled resources to high-priority tasks.

- Correct Answer: B

108. **The primary goal of 'Plan Stakeholder Engagement' is to:**

- A) Identify all potential stakeholders of the project.

- B) Document the interests of all parties affected by the project.

- C) Develop approaches to involve stakeholders based on their needs, expectations, and potential impact.

- D) Assign roles and responsibilities to stakeholders.

- Correct Answer: C

109. **'Quantitative Risk Analysis' should be performed when:**

- A) The project is small and involves minimal risk.

- B) Detailed analysis is required to understand the impact of risks on project objectives.

- C) The project manager decides it is necessary, regardless of project size or complexity.

- D) Only at the beginning of the project for initial risk assessment.

- Correct Answer: B

110.   In 'Project Quality Management', the 'Cost of Non-Conformance' refers to:

- A) The budget allocated for quality training programs.

- B) Expenses related to quality control measures and testing.

- C) Costs incurred from not meeting quality requirements, including rework and scrap.

- D) The total amount spent on quality audits.

- Correct Answer: C

111.   The 'Direct and Manage Project Work' process includes:

- A) Creating change requests as necessary.

- B) Approving or rejecting change requests.

- C) Updating the project management plan.

- D) Performing the work defined in the project management plan.

- Correct Answer: D

112.   'Manage Communications' process is critical for:

- A) Documenting project progress and performance to ensure stakeholders are always informed.

- B) Establishing the project's information distribution framework.

- C) Generating, collecting, distributing, storing, retrieving, and disposing of project information according to the plan.

- D) Selecting the appropriate communication technology for the project.

- Correct Answer: C

113.   The main objective of 'Monitor Stakeholder Engagement' is to:

- A) Continually identify new stakeholders throughout the project.

- B) Ensure stakeholders' expectations are met by adjusting strategies and plans as necessary.

- C) Update the stakeholder register and engagement strategies.

- D) Limit stakeholder interaction to control project scope.

- Correct Answer: B

114.   'Analogous Estimating' is most effective when:

- A) There is a vast amount of detailed information about the current project.

- B) The project is similar to past projects, and historical data can be used for estimation.

- C) A high degree of accuracy is not required.

- D) The project team prefers not to use complex statistical methods.

- Correct Answer: B

115. In the 'Perform Integrated Change Control' process, the Change Control Board (CCB) is responsible for:

- A) Implementing changes approved by the project manager.

- B) Reviewing, evaluating, and approving or rejecting change requests.

- C) Directly making changes to the project scope.

- D) Documenting changes in the project charter.

- Correct Answer: B

116. 'Plan Communications Management' aims to produce a document that:

- A) Lists all project stakeholders and their contact information.

- B) Details how project information will be disseminated to stakeholders.

- C) Specifies the project team's communication preferences.

- D) Outlines the project's document management system.

- Correct Answer: B

117. Performing 'Quantitative Risk Analysis' involves techniques such as:

- A) SWOT Analysis to identify strengths, weaknesses, opportunities, and threats.

- B) Monte Carlo simulations to analyze the impact of risks on project objectives.

- C) Brainstorming sessions to generate a comprehensive list of project risks.

- D) Checklists derived from historical project data to ensure all potential risks are considered.

- Correct Answer: B

118. 'Control Costs' focuses on:

- A) Establishing the project's budget during the initial planning phase.

- B) Monitoring the status of the project to update the cost forecasts and manage changes to the cost baseline.

- C) Reducing the overall project costs by cutting non-essential activities.

- D) Increasing the project budget to cover identified risks.

- Correct Answer: B

119. 'Monitor and Control Project Work' is primarily concerned with:

- A) Making changes to the project management plan and project documents.

- B) Tracking, reviewing, and reporting on overall project progress to meet performance objectives.

- C) Directly managing the project tasks and deliverables.

- D) Communicating project status to external stakeholders exclusively.

- Correct Answer: B

120. **In 'Earned Value Management' (EVM), 'Planned Value' (PV) represents:**

- A) The value of work actually accomplished to date.

- B) The authorized budget assigned to the scheduled work.

- C) The total costs incurred for the work completed.

- D) The estimated value of work not yet started.

- Correct Answer: B

121. **The 'Manage Quality' process aims to:**

- A) Ensure project deliverables conform to customer requirements and fit for purpose.

- B) Focus exclusively on the final product's quality, not the quality of project management processes.

- C) Address only the costs associated with ensuring quality.

- D) Implement the organization's quality policies, objectives, and responsibilities so that the project will satisfy the needs for which it was undertaken.

- Correct Answer: D

122. **The 'Direct and Manage Project Work' process is critical for:**

- A) Only initiating activities at the start of the project.

- B) Implementing the project management plan and producing the project's deliverables.

- C) Monitoring and reporting project progress to stakeholders.

- D) Approving budget adjustments and additional funding.

- Correct Answer: B

123. **'Plan Stakeholder Engagement' results in the development of:**

- A) A stakeholder register that lists all project stakeholders.

- B) A detailed project scope statement.

- C) A stakeholder engagement plan that outlines strategies to engage stakeholders effectively.

- D) A communication plan detailing information distribution.

- Correct Answer: C

124. **In the context of 'Project Cost Management', 'Life Cycle Costing':**

- A) Considers only the costs incurred during the project execution phase.

- B) Involves estimating the total costs associated with the project from initiation through maintenance and disposal.

- C) Is a technique used exclusively during the 'Control Costs' process.

- D) Focuses on reducing the project's capital expenditure during the initiation phase.

- Correct Answer: B

125.   The primary function of 'Monitor Risks' is to:

- A) Eliminate all project risks.

- B) Track identified risks, monitor residual risks, re-assess existing risks, and identify new risks throughout the project lifecycle.

- C) Develop new risk response strategies for all identified risks.

- D) Allocate additional budget to cover potential risks identified in the risk register.

- Correct Answer: B

126.   The 'Monitor Risks' process is essential because it:

- A) Ensures that no new risks are identified during the project lifecycle.

- B) Continuously tracks identified risks, monitors residual risks, and identifies new risks, keeping the risk management plan updated.

- C) Focuses solely on eliminating all project risks.

- D) Deals with requesting additional funds to cover unforeseen risks.

- Correct Answer: B

127.   'Resource Optimization Techniques' are utilized in schedule management to:

- A) Ensure that project resources are expended as quickly as possible to speed up project completion.

- B) Address resource allocation and leveling concerns, potentially affecting project timelines while optimizing resource use.

- C) Increase the project budget to allow for the acquisition of additional resources.

- D) Reduce the quality of resources used in order to decrease project costs.

- Correct Answer: B

128.   In the 'Develop Project Charter' process, a key element is:

- A) Outlining the detailed project budget.

- B) Defining high-level project and product requirements.

- C) Specifying all project milestones and deliverables.

- D) Assigning specific tasks to project team members.

- Correct Answer: B

129. **The 'Perform Qualitative Risk Analysis' process is critical for projects because it:**

- A) Provides a numerical probability and impact rating of risks.

- B) Helps prioritize risks for further analysis or action by assessing their probability of occurrence and impact on project objectives.

- C) Eliminates the need for a 'Quantitative Risk Analysis'.

- D) Directly leads to the development of the project risk management plan.

- Correct Answer: B

130. **'Earned Value Management' (EVM) is an effective tool for:**

- A) Tracking only the physical performance of the project without considering costs.

- B) Providing project managers with early warning signs of possible schedule delays and cost overruns.

- C) Eliminating the need for a project management plan.

- D) Calculating the exact date the project will be completed and the total cost at completion.

- Correct Answer: B

131. **In 'Control Schedule', a primary technique used is:**

- A) Fast tracking to reduce the project duration.

- B) Resource leveling to balance the demand for resources with the available supply.

- C) Variance analysis to compare planned versus actual progress.

- D) Critical path method to assign resources.

- Correct Answer: C

132. **The 'Plan Procurement Management' process is designed to:**

- A) Finalize purchase orders and contracts.

- B) Identify project needs that can be best met by acquiring products or services outside the organization.

- C) Directly manage and control the relationship with vendors.

- D) Ensure that all procurements meet the technical specifications of the project.

- Correct Answer: B

133. **'Stakeholder Engagement Assessment Matrix' is a tool used to:**

- A) Record and analyze the power/interest of all stakeholders.

- B) Track and compare the current level of stakeholder engagement against the desired level.

- C) Assign and manage tasks to different stakeholders based on their interest and influence.

- D) Measure the financial impact stakeholders have on the project.

- Correct Answer: B

134. 'Quality Audits' within the 'Manage Quality' process aim to:

- A) Identify inefficiencies within the project processes.

- B) Ensure the project complies with external standards and regulations.

- C) Directly inspect project deliverables for defects.

- D) Determine the accuracy of cost estimates.

- Correct Answer: A

135. The 'Develop Project Management Plan' process integrates:

- A) All subsidiary plans and baselines into a comprehensive project management plan.

- B) Only the project schedule and costs into the project charter.

- C) Stakeholder feedback into the project scope document.

- D) Project risks into the project budget.

- Correct Answer: A

136. 'Parametric Estimating' is most effective when:

- A) The project is unique, and there is little similar historical data.

- B) The project activities have a quantifiable and statistical relationship to variables.

- C) Detailed information on the project is not yet available.

- D) Estimating activity durations rather than costs.

- Correct Answer: B

137. In 'Project Quality Management', the 'Cost of Quality' includes:

- A) Only the expenses related to fixing defects.

- B) Costs incurred through quality activities to ensure the project meets performance requirements, including prevention, appraisal, and failure costs.

- C) The total amount spent on quality control tests and inspections.

- D) The budget allocated for hiring external quality consultants.

- Correct Answer: B

138. The 'Identify Stakeholders' process is crucial for:

- A) Documenting the interests of all parties affected by the project and determining how their participation will influence the project execution.

- B) Assigning roles and responsibilities within the project team.

- C) Establishing the project's scope baseline.

- D) Developing the project budget.

- Correct Answer: A

139. 'Change Control Boards' (CCBs) are integral to which process?

- A) Perform Integrated Change Control

- B) Direct and Manage Project Work

- C) Monitor and Control Project Work

- D) Plan Risk Management

- Correct Answer: A

140. 'Work Performance Data' in project management refers to:

- A) Summaries of project progress and status.

- B) Raw observations and measurements of project activities as they are performed.

- C) The analyzed outcomes of work performance, indicating variances from the plan.

- D) The financial analysis of project expenditures.

- Correct Answer: B

141. 'Monte Carlo Simulation' in risk management is used for:

- A) Determining the project's critical path.

- B) Analyzing the effect of identified risks on the project's overall objectives.

- C) Assigning qualitative risk ratings to project risks.

- D) Identifying potential new risks.

- Correct Answer: B

142. The 'Control Communications' process is essential for ensuring:

- A) The project's communication methods are efficient and effective.

- B) All project communications occur in real-time.

- C) Stakeholders have unlimited access to project information.

- D) Communication technologies are state-of-the-art.

- Correct Answer: A

143. In the context of 'Project Schedule Management', 'crashing' is a technique used to:

- A) Decrease the amount of work by removing unnecessary tasks.

- B) Reduce the project duration by adding additional resources to critical path activities.

- C) Extend the project schedule to reduce the workload on resources.

- D) Improve the accuracy of activity duration estimates.

- Correct Answer: B

144. The 'Plan Stakeholder Engagement' process results in:

- A) A detailed list of project stakeholders and their contact information.

- B) A dynamic plan outlining how to engage stakeholders and adjust strategies based on project evolution and stakeholder feedback.

- C) A static document that outlines initial stakeholder expectations.

- D) An organizational chart that includes all project stakeholders.

- Correct Answer: B

145. 'Analogous Estimating' relies on:

- A) The detailed analysis of each component of the project.

- B) The use of project management software to calculate estimates.

- C) Historical data from similar projects as the basis for estimates.

- D) Statistical relationships between historical data and project variables.

- Correct Answer: C

146. During 'Perform Integrated Change Control', the main responsibility of the Change Control Board (CCB) is to:

- A) Implement changes approved by the project manager.

- B) Review, approve, or reject change requests.

- C) Directly manage changes on the project site.

- D) Ensure that all change requests are documented in the project charter.

- Correct Answer: B

147. 'Plan Communications Management' aims to:

- A) Document the rules for project communications.

- B) Establish the information and communications needs of the stakeholders.

- C) Ensure that communication within the project team is limited to essential information.

- D) Set up the project's social media communication channels.

- Correct Answer: B

148. 'Quantitative Risk Analysis' involves tools and techniques such as:

- A) SWOT Analysis.

- B) Monte Carlo simulations and decision tree analysis.

- C) Expert judgment and interviews.

- D) Stakeholder surveys and focus groups.

- Correct Answer: B

149.   In 'Control Costs', a key practice is:

- A) Approving all expenditures as they occur to ensure project progress.

- B) Monitoring the status of the project to update the cost forecast.

- C) Continuously increasing the budget to meet evolving project needs.

- D) Reducing project costs by cutting project scope.

- Correct Answer: B

150.   'Monitor and Control Project Work' is significant because it:

- A) Directly involves completing the project work as per the project management plan.

- B) Involves tracking, reviewing, and reporting project progress to meet performance objectives.

- C) Is focused solely on managing the project team and their tasks.

- D) Entails communicating project status only to external stakeholders.

- Correct Answer: B

151.   Effective project integration management primarily ensures that:

- A) Project tasks are executed in isolation to meet specific objectives.

- B) Various elements of the project are properly coordinated.

- C) The project is completed within the allocated budget.

- D) Stakeholder communication is prioritized over project tasks.

- Correct Answer: B

152.   The 'Develop Project Charter' process is essential because it:

- A) Authorizes the project manager to apply organizational resources to project activities.

- B) Defines the project's detailed scope, budget, and schedule.

- C) Establishes the project team and assigns tasks.

- D) Outlines the project's communication plan.

- Correct Answer: A

153.   In 'Project Scope Management', the 'Create WBS' (Work Breakdown Structure) process is crucial for:

- A) Identifying and documenting the project's specific activities.

- B) Breaking down project deliverables into smaller, more manageable components.

141

- C) Establishing a timeline for project deliverables.

- D) Allocating budget to individual project tasks.

- Correct Answer: B

154. 'Quantitative Risk Analysis':

- A) Provides a prioritized list of risks based on impact.

- B) Assigns numerical values to the probability and impact of project risks.

- C) Should be conducted before qualitative risk analysis.

- D) Focuses solely on the negative impacts of project risks.

- Correct Answer: B

155. The 'Control Schedule' process involves:

- A) Developing the project schedule.

- B) Determining the project's critical path.

- C) Monitoring the status of project activities to update project progress and manage changes to the schedule baseline.

- D) Assigning resources to scheduled activities.

- Correct Answer: C

156. 'Manage Stakeholder Engagement' is a process that:

- A) Is completed once at the start of the project.

- B) Involves continuous communication and negotiation with stakeholders to meet their needs and address issues as they arise.

- C) Focuses exclusively on collecting requirements from stakeholders.

- D) Is only necessary for external stakeholders.

- Correct Answer: B

157. Which technique is NOT a part of the 'Estimate Activity Durations' process?

- A) Parametric estimating

- B) Analogous estimating

- C) Monte Carlo simulation

- D) Critical Path Method (CPM)

- Correct Answer: D

158. 'Perform Integrated Change Control' ensures that:

- A) All changes are approved without review to expedite the project.

142

- B) Changes to the project are reviewed, approved, or rejected to manage their impact on the project.

- C) No changes are allowed once the project plan is baselined.

- D) Only the project manager has the authority to approve changes.

- Correct Answer: B

159.   The purpose of 'Plan Communications Management' is to:

- A) Document the project's escalation process for resolving issues.

- B) Ensure that project information is timely and appropriately disseminated among stakeholders.

- C) Define roles and responsibilities for project communication.

- D) Establish the project's document management system.

- Correct Answer: B

160.   'Qualitative Risk Analysis' is primarily conducted to:

- A) Calculate the cost implications of identified risks.

- B) Prioritize risks for further analysis or action by assessing their probability of occurrence and impact.

- C) Implement immediate risk response actions.

- D) Quantify the time implications of risks on the project schedule.

- Correct Answer: B

161.   In the 'Control Costs' process, 'Variance Analysis' is used to:

- A) Adjust the project budget to reflect changes in project scope.

- B) Determine the reason behind differences between planned and actual project costs.

- C) Allocate additional funds to high-priority project tasks.

- D) Reduce overall project costs by identifying unnecessary expenditures.

- Correct Answer: B

162.   'Monitor and Control Project Work' is crucial for:

- A) Directing the day-to-day execution of project tasks.

- B) Ensuring that project objectives are met by monitoring project performance and implementing necessary changes.

- C) Approving all project expenditures and budget adjustments.

- D) Communicating project progress to stakeholders.

- Correct Answer: B

163.   The 'Manage Quality' process includes activities that:

- A) Define the project's quality policies and procedures.

- B) Ensure the project's deliverables meet the agreed-upon standards and stakeholder expectations.

- C) Are focused solely on product testing and defect identification.

- D) Involve updating the quality management plan based on performance metrics.

- Correct Answer: B

164. 'Direct and Manage Project Work' is focused on:

- A) Updating the project management plan to reflect approved changes.

- B) Executing the work defined in the project management plan to achieve the project's objectives.

- C) Communicating with stakeholders about project progress.

- D) Identifying and documenting changes to the project scope.

- Correct Answer: B

165. The 'Develop Project Team' process aims to:

- A) Define project roles and responsibilities.

- B) Enhance project team members' skills, thereby improving team dynamics and project performance.

- C) Assign project tasks to team members based on their skills and experience.

- D) Determine the total number of team members needed for the project.

- Correct Answer: B

166. 'Plan Stakeholder Engagement' results in:

- A) A stakeholder register.

- B) A stakeholder management plan.

- C) An engagement strategy for each stakeholder.

- D) Documentation of stakeholder issues and concerns.

- Correct Answer: B

167. 'Analogous Estimating' is characterized by:

- A) High accuracy due to the use of detailed project information.

- B) Being quick and less costly but less accurate, using historical data from similar projects.

- C) Relying on statistical methods to predict project costs.

- D) Involving the entire project team for consensus-based estimating.

- Correct Answer: B

168. The 'Perform Integrated Change Control' process is significant because it:

- A) Allows for unlimited changes to the project scope without any approvals.

- B) Facilitates the evaluation of all change requests in a systematic manner, ensuring that no changes are made without proper authorization.

- C) Is solely the responsibility of the project manager, without involving any other stakeholders.

- D) Only applies to changes in the project schedule, not to scope or cost.

- Correct Answer: B

169. The 'Plan Communications Management' process is designed to:

- A) Limit the project communication to only essential information to avoid information overload.

- B) Establish a plan that outlines how project information will be shared with stakeholders, including methods, frequency, and content.

- C) Define the project's structure and flow of communication within the project team.

- D) Focus exclusively on external project communications.

- Correct Answer: B

170. 'Quantitative Risk Analysis':

- A) Is always performed for all identified risks, regardless of their impact on the project.

- B) Uses numerical methods to assess the effect of identified risks on overall project objectives, providing a basis for making decisions and establishing priorities.

- C) Involves assigning qualitative labels (such as high, medium, low) to risks based on their severity.

- D) Is conducted immediately after the project charter is approved to ensure all risks are quantified early.

- Correct Answer: B

171. The purpose of 'Control Costs' is to:

- A) Establish an initial project budget baseline that cannot be changed.

- B) Monitor project expenditures and performance against the cost baseline to manage changes and ensure that the project remains within budget.

- C) Identify new funding sources for the project when cost overruns occur.

- D) Reduce the project scope to align with the available budget.

- Correct Answer: B

172. 'Monitor and Control Project Work' includes activities such as:

- A) Directly managing the project team and its tasks.

- B) Identifying changes and recommending corrective or preventive actions based on actual performance.

- C) Developing the project management plan.

- D) Approving budget adjustments and additional funding requests.

- Correct Answer: B

173. In the 'Earned Value Management' (EVM) methodology, 'Planned Value' (PV) is:

- A) The estimated value of the work actually accomplished.

- B) The authorized budget assigned to scheduled work.

- C) The total costs incurred in accomplishing work.

- D) The value of work planned to be completed at a given time.

- Correct Answer: B

174. 'Manage Quality' focuses on:

- A) The execution of the project management plan according to the quality standards.

- B) Incorporating the organization's quality policies into the project.

- C) Continuous process improvement and embedding quality in project processes.

- D) Inspecting and correcting defects in project deliverables.

- Correct Answer: C

175. The 'Direct and Manage Project Work' process is vital for:

- A) Approving changes and updating the project management plan accordingly.

- B) Carrying out the activities necessary to produce the project's deliverables according to the project management plan.

- C) Monitoring the project team's performance against the project schedule.

- D) Communicating project progress to stakeholders.

- Correct Answer: B

176. The primary focus of 'Plan Communications Management' is to:

- A) Archive all communications for project documentation purposes.

- B) Develop a plan that outlines how, when, and by whom information will be administered and disseminated.

- C) Determine the project's organizational structure and reporting relationships.

- D) Specify the types of communication media to be used on the project.

- Correct Answer: B

177. 'Quantitative Risk Analysis' is particularly important for:

- A) Projects with a fixed budget and no flexibility for cost overruns.

- B) Understanding the probability and impact of risks in numerical terms to aid in decision making and contingency planning.

- C) Early stages of the project when specific risks are not yet identified.

- D) Small projects where risks can be easily managed without detailed analysis.

- Correct Answer: B

178. The purpose of 'Control Costs' is to:

- A) Establish the budget baseline against which project performance can be monitored and controlled.

- B) Ensure that every change to the project budget is recorded and reflected in the cost baseline.

- C) Monitor project expenditure and performance against the cost baseline to manage changes to the cost baseline.

- D) Reduce the costs associated with the project to increase profitability.

- Correct Answer: C

179. 'Monitor and Control Project Work' is vital for:

- A) Direct intervention and management of the project tasks by the project manager.

- B) Ensuring that work is being performed according to the project management plan and making adjustments as necessary.

- C) The development and execution of the project management plan.

- D) Communication of project progress to external stakeholders.

- Correct Answer: B

180. In the context of 'Earned Value Management' (EVM), 'Planned Value' (PV) refers to:

- A) The work scheduled to be completed by a certain date and its associated budget.

- B) The total cost incurred to achieve a particular stage of work.

- C) The value of work actually completed to date compared to the budget.

- D) The estimated total cost of the project at completion.

- Correct Answer: A

Conclusion

As we come to the end of this comprehensive guide to PMP certification preparation, it's important to reflect on the journey we've undertaken together. Throughout this book, we've delved into the intricacies of project management, exploring fundamental concepts, advanced techniques, and real-world case studies. Now, as you prepare to embark on your own PMP certification journey, let's recap some key takeaways and reflect on the significance of this knowledge.

Reflection on Learning:

Throughout this journey, we've traversed a vast landscape of project management concepts and methodologies, each chapter serving as a building block in the construction of your expertise. From the foundational understanding of key terms to the intricate exploration of agile methodologies and procurement management, every section has added layers to your comprehension, fostering a holistic view of project management.

As you engaged with the material, delving into exercises and case studies, you didn't just passively absorb information; you actively participated in your own learning. This active engagement has not only deepened your knowledge but also sharpened your critical thinking and problem-solving abilities. These skills are not just academic exercises; they are the very tools that will empower you to navigate the complexities of real-world projects with confidence and efficacy.

Preparation for Success:

Beyond theoretical understanding, this guide has armed you with practical strategies and techniques essential for success in both the PMP certification exam and your future endeavors as a project manager. Whether it's the art of crafting effective communication strategies to foster collaboration, the science of mitigating project risks through strategic planning, or the moral compass needed to navigate ethical dilemmas with integrity, you now possess a versatile toolkit honed for the challenges ahead.

But this preparation is not merely about passing an exam; it's about readiness for the dynamic and unpredictable terrain of project management. The strategies outlined in this guide are not static solutions but adaptable frameworks designed to meet the ever-evolving demands of the field. Armed with this knowledge, you are not just a student preparing for a test; you are a proficient practitioner equipped to lead projects to success in the real world.

Empowerment and Confidence:

As the date of your PMP exam approaches, it's crucial to recognize the depth of preparation you've undertaken. You've immersed yourself in the intricacies of project management, absorbing knowledge and honing skills that are vital for success. As you stand on the threshold of the exam room, remember that you are not entering uncharted territory; you are stepping into an arena where your preparation and determination will be your greatest assets.

Have confidence in your abilities. Trust in the foundation you've built through diligent study and engagement with this guide. Every concept you've grasped, every technique you've mastered, and every insight you've gained has equipped you for the challenges ahead. Approach the exam not with trepidation, but with the assurance that you possess the knowledge and skills necessary to excel.

Yet, it's essential to remember that success on the PMP exam is not just about earning a passing score. It's about demonstrating your proficiency and readiness to lead and manage projects effectively in the real world. The exam is a validation of your capabilities, a milestone on your journey to becoming a certified Project Management Professional. So, embrace the opportunity to showcase your expertise and rise to the occasion with confidence.

Continued Growth:

The culmination of your PMP exam is not the end of your journey—it's just the beginning. Becoming a certified Project Management Professional is not merely about acquiring a credential; it's a commitment to continuous learning and professional development. As you celebrate your achievement, remember that there is always more to learn, new skills to acquire, and fresh insights to gain.

Stay curious. Keep exploring emerging trends and best practices in project management. The field is constantly evolving, and staying abreast of the latest developments will ensure that you remain at the forefront of your profession. Seek out opportunities for growth, whether through advanced certifications, specialized training programs, or participation in professional communities.

But beyond personal advancement, remember the broader impact you can make as a Project Management Professional. Each project you undertake is an opportunity to make a positive difference—to deliver value to stakeholders, empower teams, and drive organizational success. Approach every project with passion and purpose, knowing that your expertise can shape outcomes and create lasting change.

So, as you embark on this next phase of your journey, do so with a commitment to excellence, a thirst for knowledge, and a dedication to making a difference. The world of project management awaits your continued growth and contributions. Embrace the opportunities that lie ahead, and let your journey as a certified Project Management Professional be defined not by where you've been, but by where you're headed.

Acknowledgments:

Before you embark on the next chapter of your journey, I want to take a moment to express my heartfelt gratitude to all those who have contributed to the creation of this guide. This book is not the work of a single individual but the collaborative effort of many dedicated individuals whose insights, expertise, and support have been invaluable.

First and foremost, I extend my deepest appreciation to the authors and experts whose knowledge and experience have shaped the content of this guide. Their commitment to excellence in project management has been the driving force behind the creation of this resource, and their contributions have enriched its depth and breadth.

I also want to thank the readers whose engagement and feedback have fueled the purpose of this book. Your curiosity, questions, and insights have inspired us to continually strive for clarity, relevance, and effectiveness in conveying complex concepts and practical strategies.

To the mentors, colleagues, and peers who have offered guidance, encouragement, and support along the way, I am profoundly grateful. Your wisdom, encouragement, and belief in the value of this endeavor have been a constant source of inspiration and motivation.

As you close this book and prepare to embark on the next phase of your journey, remember that the principles and lessons you've learned here are not mere words on a page; they are guiding lights illuminating your path towards success in project management. Carry them with you as you navigate the challenges and opportunities that lie ahead, and let them serve as a compass guiding you towards excellence.

Go forth with confidence, curiosity, and a commitment to making a difference. The world of project management awaits your leadership, and I have every confidence that you will rise to the occasion and make a meaningful impact.

Best of luck on your PMP certification journey! May your dedication, perseverance, and passion for excellence propel you to new heights of success.

Made in the USA
Middletown, DE
09 September 2024

60521692R00084